Breath of Kenya

A Missionary Journal

Charles Herrick

Library of Congress Number 5-739-512

ISBN: 0 – 972 – 97619 – 1

Printed in Canada

Human Fabric
Publishing

Seattle

To Kristy
The specialest wife that could ever be

We two are one and whenever we are apart
I feel the strain on my soul and my psyche.

My missionary work often leads me into
Some pretty scary places.
Sometimes I have a sense of dread
And I fear I may not make it back.

"What am I doing here?" I ask myself. "What's
the point? Who am I kidding?"

Then a small child grasps my hand and the father
Looks at me and asks with his eyes,
"Can you help?"

Lord, give me the wisdom to balance the
Stewardship of my wonderful marriage
With the compassion for the suffering
And the poor.

Never again will they hunger;
never again will they thirst
The sun will not beat upon them,
nor any scorching heat …

He will lead them to springs of living water.
And God will wipe away every tear from their eyes

Revelations
Chapter 7

ACKNOWLEDGEMENTS

I praise God for the opportunity to have my life changed in a way that was wonderfully painful and lasting. I now have ever so much more to be thankful for and so much less do I seek *things* to complete and complement what He has already given me.

I thank my wife who never doubted and was always wise in her advice. Neither of us sleeps well when I'm gone because we two really are one. She's delicate but brave. In heaven I pray she'll be able to do one whole pull-up.

I thank the wonderful African family of Christopher Sure: Florence, Isaiah, Calvince, little Flo and Angela. Their patience with the strange white man who never seemed to sleep was only exceeded by their love and warmth.

I thank Priscilla Larsen who directs our church missionary activities at Pine Lake Covenant. A missionary daughter herself, she never forgot her roots and somehow finds missionary opportunities all over the world. Perhaps it's because she is looking for them and perhaps God just knows she's an incurable Mom with ever open arms.

I thank soft spoken Dr. Ralph Aye, one of Seattle's leading thoracic surgeons. He prepared me mentally for what I would encounter. A couple of the pictures I used in the center of the book were taken by him. He's a gifted, articulate man whose humble walk has forced me to think about my own comportment. He has helped me distinguish between a believer and a follower of the One who heals all.

I thank all the people who have read this book and encouraged me. Drafts of it appear to be in circulation all over Earth since I get emails now and then from surgeons in Chicago and executives in Europe. I don't know how you got the book but thanks for the encouragement and critique.

I thank John Woods, author, artist and musician who helped me with the set up and layout and who gently encouraged me to take the right steps toward publication. He's a very wise man.

And thanks to Bullard, my Bulldog, who didn't do the typical dog guilt thing when I returned.

Contents

Breath of Kenya

Chapter One

I will never look at life the same way.

Chapter Two
Leaving Here

On a steely cold morning in February, I stepped onto the rubberized running track of a high school in one of the affluent suburban neighborhoods surrounding Seattle. I looked at the sky as I leaned against the fence and stretched my calf muscles, preparing them this last day for the hills of western Kenya. As I put my gloves on to start my intervals I could see my breath and I was thankful that I would soon be where it was warm and sunny, only a few miles from the equator in Africa.

I did not know that I would be entering a war zone in almost every respect except for the bullets. It would be complete with conditions of extreme deprivation, enemies both spiritual and physical and of course, people dying in every direction all around me. And then, like a war zone, there would be adventure, people of character, light-hearted moments, insights and exploits of unexpected philosophers, veterans and heroes.

These times in the early morning at the track were more than just physical training exercises. I took advantage of the solitude and, to a degree, the pain of these workouts to speak at length with God. Today I had a lot to say. And I hoped to hear some answers to some very tough questions.

My greatest fear was that I would let God down on my first missionary effort and thereby fail to serve effectively the people of Kodera, the troubled village where I was to live for so many weeks. I had chosen as my theme for this endeavor, Genesis 41:16, wherein Joseph is brought up out of prison to interpret Pharaoh's strange dream. Joseph had developed a reputation for being able to divine dreams and now he was brought into a critical test of those abilities. When Pharaoh said in verse 15: "I had a dream, and no one can interpret it. But I have heard it said of you that when you hear a dream, you can interpret it." Joseph responded by saying what would become my watchword: "I cannot do it… but God will…"

Those first four words had been hard for me to say. I had had a history of success in business, academics, art, sports, etc. I had led a blessed life and now I was to confront something so much bigger than I could handle. I would see myself simply as one of the soldiers in an effort that was truly a battle; where daily the presence of evil hung in the air and behind every mud hut in a village with no apparent means of defense.

I did my two and half mile warm up and then proceeded to run the stairs in preparation for some 400 meter speed intervals. I did that 12 times and then warmed down for a mile. Half way through such an intense workout, the cold air would become my friend - a source of great relief.

Toward the end of the run, the temperature dipped and the horizon darkened. Rain was not far off. Since this was my last full day in town, I felt it appropriate to ask God once more, in all sincerity, "Is this something you really want me to do?"

As I asked this question, I rounded the far turn and despite the prevailing temperature of approximately 35 degrees Fahrenheit, a warm wind swept over me which had to be almost 80 degrees. This, I felt, was my final call from far away. This was the breath of Kenya.

My wife and daughter accompanied me to the airport. Women have the ability to provide support in the way they look at you and the way they further soften their words as you set out on your endeavor. Their support is given so unreservedly that it dulls the edges of your own misgivings. If you were advising yourself, there would be plenty of reservations. Women support you unreservedly because it reflects a feminine code of honor. It should serve as a reminder that your love for your wife and for your daughters should be given unreservedly as well.

Walking through the parking garage and then through the airport terminal, there was less and less to say at a time when I wanted to say so much. Something told me that almost any words would be inadequate. I prayed simply that God would protect them while I was gone and that he would somehow communicate to them and remind them in my absence how much I loved them. They meant so much to me.

As I descended the escalator I looked back at them. For days I had seen the change coming over my wife as she prepared herself to face the longest time we would ever be apart. Men, as undeserving as we are, are blessed by the inexplicable, abiding loyalty women have for their mates. It struck me for the first time that this was indeed a painful burden women bear. It was first recorded briefly in Genesis, with Moses possibly unaware of what he was writing when God said to Eve, "Your desire will be for your husband."

I hate Seattle's weather nine months of the year. So many times in the past I had said to Kristy, "Let's move to Montana," or "Let's move to Costa Rica, or India or Kenya…" Although I am one of the increasingly rare Seattleites who was actually born there, I have never gotten used to the rain and I have often dreamed of being anywhere else. This perennial search for better climes is a bit irritating to Kristy who loves her 5 acre homestead in the middle of a bustling suburb. She likes the American domestic life and Seattle is just fine.

Now I was leaving. I couldn't help but feel remorse. I was rewarding a woman's love and loyalty by heading off to a country that had developed a nasty reputation for corruption, health problems, poverty and worse. Only three weeks prior, Christopher, the husband of the family I was supposed to stay with in this remote region, was under threat of death from three men in his village. He had been told of the plot to kill him by an informant. It seemed these men were not getting their normal slice of graft from the progressive efforts Christopher was introducing. When he learned of the threat, he sent a plaintive note to those of us who knew him back in the Seattle area.

The question arose regarding my planned trip to Kenya. Should I cancel it or at least postpone it? Equally troubling was the dilemma of whether I should be telling my wife about the threats made to

Christopher. This was a prayerfully tough question. Should I burden her with something over which she would have no control once I hopped aboard the airplane? Do I act as if everything is all right while the death-threat remains? My wife and I had never lied to one another. The trust developed in the years of preserving that record was something I was not going to abandon under any circumstances.

I sent a memo back to Christopher. I described a similar, horrifying situation I was once in. I explained to Christopher that this was the time to separate Christian behavior from what *feels* like the right response. Treat them lovingly, I advised. Forgive them and pray earnestly for their well being. He applied this advice, which I pulled right out of the Sermon on the Mount. God intervened.

The first man got stuck in Nairobi with no means of getting back home. Somehow he came across Christopher in that city of 3 million people and Christopher gave him a ride all the way across Kenya to their village. The next man found Christopher's son being invited to his own son's birthday party because the two had recently become close friends at school. The third man ran into a serious financial issue. The school he had worked so long to get his daughter into was demanding he pay on the deadline or the slot would go to the next student in a very long line. He would not have the money until the day after. Christopher provided him the loan he needed to the family's great relief. The danger was rapidly passing.

I was going to Kenya.

The escalator moved slowly. I looked down for just a moment at the crowd of unsmiling, international travelers accumulating at the checkpoint to S gate. And then I looked up. My wife and daughter were gone from sight. The last glimpse I had had of them, the two brilliant women in my life, was a glimmer of light from tears welling in their eyes.

I closed my eyes and the tears ran to the end of my eyelashes and hung there battling gravity while I wrestled with a surge of indecision. The escalator deposited me on the landing and my trip to Kenya began.

Chapter Three
Getting There

If you land at Kenyatta Airport, at some point you will have to drive through Nairobi. Nairobi to a Westerner is not a pretty place. It is a city of three million people, three quarters of which are beneath the classification of desperately poor. It has lots of people walking everywhere and lots of traffic yet it has no traffic lights anywhere. Somehow traffic moves pretty well using only roundabouts. Formerly a British colony, driving is supposed to be on the left in Kenya but that appears to be a general guideline as opposed to a hard requirement.

I arrived late. Ahead of me was a long drive across the semi-arid region of the country; so I spent a couple of nights at the Fairview Inn. This is a family run hotel in the middle of downtown Nairobi, but once you weave your way through the concrete barriers in front of the Israeli Embassy across the street and enter the hotel compound, you would swear you were out in the country. At $72 US with a huge breakfast buffet included, I knew I was going to like prices in Kenya. I later met with the current director and got a quick history of the inn. His grandfather came from Poland in the 40's and bought the original inn. The family has operated it ever since. This third generation manager did his undergraduate work in Boston and then got his Masters at the University of Chicago. He had a refreshingly American attitude about service and management.

On Friday I had four appointments, which took me all over and around Nairobi. In the morning I went to the African Council of Churches complex and met with a key Anglican operation that was involved in well-organized relief work throughout Kenya. Then I met with both Kenyatta University and Jomo Kenyatta University agricultural technology departments. Finally, I had dinner with George Baiden the country manager for ADRA, the massive relief organization run by the Seventh Day Adventists. This is possibly the most powerful Non-Governmental Organization (NGO) providing aid to Kenya.

George was a delightful individual whose prior assignment was as ADRA country manager for Ghana in West Africa. When we got through with the discussion of Kodera village and what kind of help I anticipated we would need, I asked him what his life was like in Africa. He told me one story, which I later found to be just a variation on what is a theme for all Africans. It appears that frequently Africans in every economic stratum are regularly forced to make decisions between bad and horrible alternatives. They might not internalize the drama inherent in movies like *Sophie's Choice;* although sadly, such choices are routine.

One of George's daughters had been attending nursing school in Nigeria. When George got reassigned to Kenya, she was to transfer to a University in the Nairobi area. She hopped aboard a bus and was on her way when the bus in front of hers suddenly came to a stop. Armed rebel gunmen went through the first bus while other gunmen held her bus at rifle point. These highwaymen had learned that the son of one the government's ministers was on board the bus.

They ordered everyone from the first bus to get off and lie face down. No one was to look up. Unfortunately, some people could not hold off their curious impulses and they raised their heads, slightly. Four people were immediately executed by pistol shot to the head. The rebels found who they were looking for and took the young man hostage. No one has seen him since.

George's daughter saw this whole thing and was greatly relieved to be leaving Nigeria. Once in Nairobi however, she was unable to make the transfer to a Kenyan college. She had to agree to lose up to two years in her pursuit of a degree or head back to Nigeria immediately and enter the fall class. That night she was back on a bus and now lives alone and away from her family in a Nigerian dorm less than 5 miles from where she witnessed the execution of innocent bus riders. This was not the last of the many painful choices I would see people being forced to make in Kenya.

While driving around Nairobi, I noticed that every hotel, every business and every restaurant had a gated, secured entrance with one or two full time security guards. You never just drove into a parking lot. There was always someone to ask you why you were there.

Why are you here at this grocery store?'

"Umm, to buy groceries?"

Brief conversation with the other security guard.

"Ok. You can come in." A similar conversation will occur at restaurants. The answer is "to eat." I have answers for virtually all Kenyan establishments by now.

The only time I drew a blank was later on when I had been in Kenya for quite a while. The guard outside of a filthy little general merchandise store approached me and asked. "Why are you here?"

"In Kenya?" I asked.

He conferred with the other guard.

"Yes."

"I sometimes wonder." I mused aloud.

Another conference.

"Ok, you can come in."

After I parked outside of a government building in one section of Nairobi, I decided to go over and talk to the two security guards. Their names were Phillip and Joseph. Phillip was a Luo from the area in western Kenya I was going to visit and Joseph was of the Kisii tribe. The Kisii territory actually neighbors Kodera. These two tribes do not get along but I sensed that was a sentiment that was shed as soon as you got to Nairobi. Nairobi was originally Kikuyu territory, but now was a melting pot (maybe more a salad bowl) of every tribe in Kenya.

I asked Phillip, a man of approximately 6 feet in height who probably weighed 130 lbs, why he was here in Nairobi and not back home in the rural west of Kenya. This is his story:

He came here when it was time for his father to divide the land among several brothers. There was simply not enough to go around – less than a half acre each from which he and the others would have to feed their families. He and a couple of his brothers had to leave. He now lives in Madera North, one of the slums of Nairobi.

What's it like? It's not like one of our slums. One of our slums in a city like Chicago would be considered a middle class urban housing neighborhood in Nairobi. However, it would be well maintained by the Kenyans who had worked hard to attain such housing. It would be a source of pride. Many steps down from an American slum, the gray horror called Madera North was built the way kids build cities with playing cards. Thin-walled units, eight by eight foot, composed of sheet metal, roofed in sheet metal. The floors are dirt. There are wall openings but no glass and often no door. You pay 5 shillings (7 cents) to use the toilet. This is too rich for many people so they often use plastic bags and toss them in a ditch or on a roof. There is no running water in the units but there is a rusty faucet here and there. There is of course no electricity. At dusk, you enter your domicile and wait out the night. It's kind of like a camping out party organized by Satan.

People live their whole lives here. They marry, have children (typically five or more) and see their surviving children marry and settle in their own eight by eight. Their children play games on mounds and in ditches and hang around until their teen years and then many head for the city to become street kids. This practice is being discouraged so we may see more children hanging around the slums. They do go to school. By the way, slum-centered schools are surprisingly well attended with many students scoring high on their state exams. They recognize this is the only way out.

I asked Phillip why he was so thin. He said he didn't eat every day. Sometimes other things came up and he had to choose between medicine or clothing or food. He said his plan was to save his money and then return to western Kenya to buy a farm of his own. He figured he had to save about 40,000 Kenyan schillings ($550 US) in order to buy a small farm.

When I mentioned this conversation to other Kenyans, they all had the same response, "He will never leave the Nairobi slums." When I asked why not, they all said he was going to get into a routine and would be unwilling to leave the easy life of a security guard for the hard work of a farm, even if his wife(s) did most of the work. In other words, why should he?

(!!!!!\!\\\\\\\!\!\\\

As the afternoon made its way into dusk, we were re-entering the city from our visit to a pump project sponsored by Kenyatta University. We drove through the financial district, which is a bit nicer than most of downtown. The crowds on the sidewalk were fairly thick with people making their way to the various public transportation alternatives: bad, worse and scary bad.

Driving slowly, we came near one of the municipal buildings. The crowd looked thicker and more active. We drove just past it and I could see they were beating someone on the sidewalk. Several people were hitting and kicking this individual and not in a casual way. These were hard hits; solid hits. The man was no longer covering himself and still they kept on with the drubbing.

"What's going on?" I asked my driver in horror as we began to merge into traffic at the roundabout.

"Mob justice," was the quick, unemotional response.

"But they appear to be killing him."

"If he's not dead already he will be. He stole a purse or something. I see it all the time."

"Don't the police ever intervene?"

"Sometimes. It's not a big thing."

It's a human being."

"Was a human being."

I looked back as one particularly large, well-dressed man stepped forward and kicked the man in the back of the head so hard I thought it would roll off and get stuck under our car. I felt nauseous. I quit looking. I would later see one other incident of mob justice in Kenya in the high desert on the way to Mombassa. That time I watched as a dozen locals escorted a terrified man across the highway, threw him down in the dirt and beat him to death in "less than" ten minutes. I'm drawing on a statistically invalid sample size but I'm thinking that "mob" and "justice" don't really belong together in the same sentence and certainly not in the context of Kenya.

The next morning we took care of a few loose ends and then headed inland for western Kenya and the village of Kodera. We stopped in the town of Nakuru for the evening. After checking in, I walked over to the market area to find a writing pad. On the way back it was going from dusk to dark and I realized it was not smart being in somewhat rough company as I passed through the various stall areas making my way back to the highway and the hotel.

As I passed through a small vacant field, a young boy yelled something and waved at me. I was being escorted by a hotel bellman who had volunteered to take me to the market. I asked why the boy was waving at me.

"He is with his mother. Her husband died and the whole family left the village for some reason. He probably wants money." I looked over and saw the mother shush him and he sat down. She was nursing a baby as they sat around a trash fire.

"Are they safe?" I asked.

"Does it look safe?" he responded. I reached in my pocket and pulled out a 1000 schilling note.

"Please take this to her," I asked of him.

"Let's get you a little closer to the hotel then and please don't pull out money like that. It's not wise. Not out here."

As we got to the part of the highway across from the hotel he saw that I was okay so he turned and trotted toward the family. He was back before I entered the hotel.

"Did you give it to her?"

"Yes."

"Did she say anything?"

"She said 'Thank you.'"

I looked him in the eye. A thousand shillings was a lot for a hotel bellman in Nakuru, too. I was definitely going to have to sharpen my philanthropic skills. Otherwise, my gifts were going to end up in the hands of the wrong desperately poor person.

Lake Nakuru is a place I have seen several times on American television. It's where the flamingoes go on their breeding and migration route. There are approximately one and a half million of them lining the lake shore and they are all making noise. Scrooge-like Marabou storks are standing guard in case one of them limps or coughs or has a baby. They are the tidy boys who do for flamingoes what wolves do for caribou. They are purported to make the herd stronger by attacking the weak or unwary. I liken that to the notion that Jesse James made banks more secure over the course of his career. I don't see predation by wolves, Marabou or Jesse's bank robbing in God's original plan.

The rest of the park was a lot like being... well I'll say it -- I felt like I was in Africa. I saw one or two of just about everything and more than a dozen rhinoceros. I don't believe there is a proper plural for rhinoceros and that's okay. A rhino in singular is plenty. According to Hindu philosophy, you reincarnate into your next life as a rhinoceros if you were an honorable Sherman tank in your previous life.

Rhinos have seams that appear to be welded. They are very prehistoric looking. One of them was just about to cross the road as our suddenly thin and diminutive Peugeot drove past him coming out of the bush with less than six feet between us. I don't know who was more surprised, the rhino or me. I do know who was more scared.

I loved the smell of the toasted savannah grass. I loved the little warthogs running around with their stiff little tails pointing straight up. The air was sweet and hot and full of danger to any creature that didn't have a Peugeot. I could have driven around for hours more with the same fascination I had when I entered the park. But we did not want to be negotiating Kenyan back roads at night. So, with a glance back at the old Cape buffalo bulls who gave us a token charge and a snort as soon as we passed, we drove out of the African part of Africa and onto the road back to the third world.

We left the park enchanted and satisfied. We made a one hour stop in a vacant lot to have our car washed. For less than two dollars and using only one bucket of water, this amazing raggy fellow got everything clean and vacuumed. This was cleaner than any car I had taken through an American car wash. He even scrubbed the wheel wells. All the mats were removed and swept spotless. We were ready for the red dusty roads of Nyanza Province.

When we drove those final back roads I only had to get out twice reducing the weight and allowing the car to clear the rocks on the way. There were potholes everywhere. Big ones. I believe Uganda had borrowed the cement mixer and had failed to return it.

We drove through the village of Kodera and passed what appeared to be almost identical mud homes, 10 foot by 10 foot with dried grass roofs. I tried to imagine a month sleeping cheek and jowl with a family of six in one of these. As we pulled into the yard of my new African home I was relieved to see that it was a compound home. I would have my own little spot to sleep. I'm not sure the emotion was one of relief. I had too many emotions going to pick one out and favor it. I just know I was tired and hungry. I also knew - despite what both cartographers and physicists may tell you - that I was a long, long way from anywhere.

Chapter Four
Being There

According to most cartoons I watched as a child and whose authority I assert here, roosters are supposed to crow at sunrise or thereabouts. In Kenya there is a one hour shift of time – sort of a permanent daylight savings time. Sunrise occurs in equatorial Kenya at about 7 AM. However, the steroidally-enhanced, multi-larynxed mutant in our yard began his community announcements every morning at 4:20 AM.

At about 6:30 or so, I would enviously listen as *normal* roosters began their lilted wafts and I believe I heard, in accompaniment, Brahms: Variations on a Theme by Haydn, op. 56b. However, I might be mistaken. But not my rooster. Instead, he would diligently load his throat with gravel and bits of metal shavings and spray his occult cry through the indefensible, windowless hole in my room. Thus began my first morning in the village of Kodera.

The night before, we had had a brief talk with my new family. Upon arrival, we entered the small domicile and I stood back politely as husband and wife, after weeks of being apart, held their emotional reunion. They shook hands. I watched in mild horror and thought, "This is normal – on Mars." I would soon learn just how normal this really was in the land of the Luo.

When the bags were unloaded I put my suitcase on the floor next to my cot. This would be my home and I needed to get adjusted to operating in a very tight space. I also needed to get out of the habit of reaching for the light switch as I entered a room or feeling for the TV remote before climbing into bed. I laid out some essentials on the floor next to my pillow which I felt would help me in the utter darkness I would experience almost 12 hours a day.

I had brought a high-tech LCD head lamp for reading, concentrated 100% DEET for mosquitoes, a flashlight to back up my headlamp, OFF aerosol spray to back up my DEET, and Purell waterless hand cleaner, jumbo economy size, so I could fend off microbial evil, should I hear it coming toward me in the night. That first night I had been shown the pit latrine and some buckets of water that were left over from the day's activities should I see the need to wash. They did not show me the sauna room, the entertainment center or the kitchen with double-door refrigerators, Jenn-air and microwave, but I figured that would be on the next day's tour.

I put on my sandals and wandered out into the Kenyan night. I stood silently looking up at a star-crowded sky -- a sky I had not seen before at the 47th parallel of the northern hemisphere. Even if this configuration were there above us, the Seattle lights and the combined afterglow of our hydroelectric abundance would have muted it on most nights. This is how stars looked when God first hung them.

There were two things related to being south of the Equator that I was bent on seeing. The first was seeing water swirl down a drain clockwise (the opposite of what it does in the northern hemisphere) and the other was seeing the Southern Cross constellation.

And there it was. It was a perfect cross just like it was supposed to be. Now if I could just find a real sink in the village, I could go home fulfilled.

By the way, weeks later, when I did find a sink, it went in whichever way I poured the water. I think it's a myth that drains swirl differently depending on the hemisphere.

The next day I was to be taken for a walking tour of the village to meet key people in my mission to help them with their economics and infrastructure. It seemed straightforward enough. I had no idea that over the course of the next several weeks, this would all start to take a strange turn and I would be spending much more time on health and medical issues. For now, it was almost silent as I used the pit latrine and then proceeded to use some leftover water to wash my strawberry blonde hair that would be sans strawberry in about two weeks of equatorial sun.

Eventually I would fall into a routine. But first I had to learn some things.

My host Christopher and I went over the day's schedule to visit various people and then go see access points to the river where I could take flow measurements for possible power generation. Everything on the agenda seemed like it was doable. In fact, it seemed we could do it all by noon. That was probably the first thing I needed to learn. I needed to disabuse myself of such notions as leaving on time, meetings as scheduled with the people I had agreed to meet, talking about the subjects we had agreed to talk about and all such little IBMisms. It would just make me crazy. It all works out. If not today, then tomorrow. Africans don't have an expression equivalent to mañana. That would be too close to committed scheduling.

When we moved to discussing the week in general, I was forced to make a decision that would more or less impact my entire visit. The following Saturday, several people in the village were going to gather in the evening and sacrifice a ram, in my honor. The thought of killing a helpless animal that was then contentedly grazing on crabgrass and old detergent boxes, somehow disturbed my view of God's natural order of things. I declared myself a vegetarian.

For those of you considering this for your trove of handy excuses, I want to point out that it's not like saying you have a cold. It is considered impolite in _all_ cultures to recover off and on from vegetarianism. When you play that card, you can't reshuffle the deck the next day.

Blonde, blue-eyed and left-handed - I had been foreign yet mentally manageable. But vegetarian was preternatural even to people whose language has no linguistic analog of preternatural. However, Africans are much better at handling disappointment than Americans. An hour later Christopher announced that in deference to my unwillingness to take a life for the temporal enjoyment of eating and celebrating he had an alternative. Instead, he would now kill a chicken.

Thus began a lengthy journey of culinary delay-and-evade that would have made Chief Joseph proud.

We made our tour of the village and spent the day meeting many wonderful people. As we walked along I observed rams and she-goats everywhere. They did not acknowledge my presence. They never looked up. Ingrates. The chickens on the other hand were on to me. They watched warily as I passed. They were trying to figure out if all white people were sellouts. I returned their stares. Observing chickens often during my stay caused me to wonder how an intelligent African man could classify such lively creatures as a vegetable.

On a day when the water in the well was more or less sufficient, I decided to do my laundry. I filled three buckets with semi-clean well-water. Kneeling in the grass on a hot sunny afternoon, I rubbed my bar of Fels-Naphtha soap on one shirt, sock or pair of underwear after another. I had previously observed laundry being done by the old lady who sometimes came by to help with chores and watch the family's disabled daughter while the mother went to the market. She spent nearly one and a half hours doing a pile of clothes. She did this every time she came over. I had watched. I was ready.

There is no washboard. Just the bucket, the bar of soap and water you hope is cleaner than your laundry. Here are some important rules:

1. Do not remove the small insect from the corner of your eye with your soapy finger.
2. Do not attempt to remove the soap from the corner of your eye with your other soapy hand.
3. Do not attempt to make it better with the back of the wrist from the first soapy hand as it too is soapy.

If you ignore these rules, you may go blind. You will deserve it and the Kenyans (viz. the old laundry lady) will just shake their heads, thinking, "Poor Mzungu. These Americans may have a lot of money but they appear to be so helpless."

But I did not need help. I trained my remaining good eye on my task and made ready for the rinse, wring and shake cycle. It's important that you wring your clothes thoroughly after soaping to reduce the water needed to rinse. As I wrung my shirt to a desiccated wafer, I noticed I was being observed with concern by the elderly laundry lady who I estimate was approaching 111 years of age.

She shook her toothless head and made her way over to where I had been enjoying myself. She took the fully wrung shirt out of my hand and mumbled something in Luo that sounded unaffirming. She then proceeded to get *another* cup-and-a-half wrung out of my shirt. She handed it back to me and once again took up her post to observe me from the shade.

I was about to feel humiliated but I took manly solace in thinking that with a couple of weeks working out in the gym I could whip her in a fair fight.

A little over one hour later, my clothes were hanging to dry.

I felt really fulfilled.

There is no way to describe each function that must be performed to get through the day in Kenya. Taken individually, they sound like a lot of work. Sewn together, it is wearying to know that it goes on every day, week after week, year after year. Add to such a day the ups and downs and occasional tragedies of life and it can hurt. It hurts to the bone just to remember.

It's such a blur now I can't recollect as clearly as I did at the end of one particularly tough day. To set music to any words you may ever hear about Africa, here is an extract of that day from my journal. It will also provide a preview of things to come:

Journal Extract: A Day in the Life of a Kenyan

The day starts early in Kenya. It's 4:00AM and I want to get up now so that I am not in the way of the other members of the family. They have never said a word but I know that my presence adds just a little onto their very heavy daily load.

I am the only white person, a Mzungu, in this village of some 1200 homes – mud huts, ten by ten foot, with a divider for sleeping and cooking on one side and dining or sitting on the other. There is no running water, no electricity. The walls are sticks and clay; the roof is baked grass. The floors are hard clay trod by hard, flat Kenyan feet.

I head for the pit latrine. It's a stall, three by three with a hole in the floor. Next to the latrine I have a bucket holding two quarts of water I saved from last night. This will be my bath. I finish just as the rooster crows at 4:20. Many had not waited for the rooster. Already as I bathed, three herds of African cattle have been driven past our yard. I can always tell, even in the dark, if it is a man or a woman driving the herd. A man takes a stick with a long rope on the end and violently beats the cattle that really don't change pace or direction that often. They are gentle and docile. They are not the spirited European stock that few here have ventured to raise. When a woman drives her cattle, she takes the same stick and taps the cattle on the shoulders, gently. The result is the same. They turn their heads slightly to acknowledge the shushing sound she makes then continue on in silence.

It will not be silent this morning. In the last few days nine people have died within a hundred yards of me. None was over 40 years of age. AIDS is the big killer here. 40% of the population is HIV positive. When it turns to full blown AIDS they go down fast. No AIDS cocktail here at 200,000 Kenya shillings a month. The rest die of various ailments: pneumonia that started with a bout with bad water and then progressed; a tumor in the stomach; a baby's first bout with malaria that went too long. People ask out of curiosity but no one really churns on the details. Death is common but nine dead in three days is a lot even for this troubled village.

The funereal ululations and drumming go late into the night. The mother of one of them wails for hours up and down the road. Her daughter died of AIDS and she talks through her tears. I tell myself what she is saying although I don't know Luo - let alone tear-clouded Luo. With one arm outstretched she is saying, almost pleading, that someone tell her how all her daughters could precede her to the grave. It wasn't this way in the old days, even the worst of the old days.

This morning the funeral processions begin with some quavering calls and a little bit of a drum beat. The father of the family I am with will attend later as many funerals as he can. For now, the family needs to get on with the day. I look up and the oldest boy has arisen as he always does about this time and has begun cranking the makeshift wooden pole that lowers the bucket into the well. It has been a long drought and he tries optimistically with the five-gallon bucket first. No chance. Now he lowers the one gallon flask with slits on each side so it can draw water while lying on its side. He raises it the 50 foot draw and then lowers it again for almost an hour and a half or until the water just won't come anymore.

With each draw he pours the cloudy water into a larger general container and a couple of two gallon basins that will be used for cooking. The water must settle for up to two hours before it is boiled for drinking or cooking. Some don't boil it and pay the price. I just saw the family of one such experiment pass by in tears.

The mother is up at 5:15. She goes about the day with surprising vigor for a woman who was up late with her sickly, deformed daughter. She smiles and says good morning with a lilt. I wave as I brush my teeth over by the fence. I hear her chopping vegetables in the kitchen. She has already lit two jikos, the little foot high charcoal stoves, 14 inches across the top. These are used for all cooking, which is done on the floor. They don't have shelves and counters. Women in Africa do most of their work on the floor with their long arms and bent back. It's a permanent picture I carry with me from Africa.

She boils water for porridge, a millet gruel the kids will drink before school. She also cuts up a papaya which came from a tree in the yard. The kids add a little milk, warm from a carton, into their porridge with a couple of scoops of brownish crystal sugar. They are clean by 7:00 or so and dressed in their uniforms. All children in Kenya, including high school students, wear uniforms in their school colors. The boys wear pants and a shirt. The girls wear a dress and a blouse. Sometimes they wear a sweater to school and continue wearing it in 95 degree weather. It makes you hot even to think about anyone in a sweater on a day like this. They are off on their walk to school, which can be as far away as three miles or more. Dust is everywhere yet they come home remarkably clean.

The mother continues on with breakfast preparation for her husband and herself and any friends that might drop by as they frequently do. People don't make appointments to see friends here and I never know whom I will be sitting with at the table .Breakfast is ready about 7:30 or 8. I purposely eat slowly to add balance on my end for her two-hour preparation. There is kale, pineapples and avocados. As a vegetarian I'm in heaven. The husband checks the pots and finds what he is looking for. It's a stew of some unknown meat, goat possibly, that was bought in the warm, open-air butchery two days ago. I pass politely on the goat.

The mother is out in the yard after breakfast washing dishes and getting ready, once the water is a little more settled, to start the three bucket laundry process that will take her one to two hours. She hangs it on the line after the final rinse. I watch her as she finally straightens up after being bent over this long. Watching her arch backward makes my back feel better. She wisely does not wring the last rinsed clothes to avoid unnecessary wrinkling.

Some of yesterday's clothes need ironing. She reaches down to the jiko and adds a couple of sticks of charcoal to her iron. Despite my warnings she continues to breathe carbon monoxide smoke from the charcoal as she irons indoors. She can either be cool and breathe poison or stay another hour out in the sun without the carbon monoxide. She chooses to be cool. I would choose neither but then I wouldn't bear the doubting looks of many if the children were to go about in wrinkled school clothes.

This family is lucky. They have a well. It's 11 AM and many women pass by with large buckets on their heads transporting water. For some this is their third one-hour round trip. Others in the village take twice as long depending on where the good water is. This village has tapped springs. Previously, they did as many villages do and dipped water out of a spring hole with a gourd and then did their settling and filtering at home. Those were dangerous times, especially during drought season.

This afternoon many of the women are making the five mile walk to the end of the road where they will catch a matatu van. The backs of these small, outfitted Japanese pickup trucks would hold four Americans. Here, they hold up to 16 Kenyans jammed in so tight I can't believe they all survive the 30 minute ride to the Kisii market place. In Kisii, the women pick up kale, now in short supply. They call it sakumu wiki, which means "push the week." It is pushed every day of the week by moms trying to get some greens into their children.

The women will spend an hour buying various items they can't get in the village. Heading back, they depart individually as they search and find matatus going to their drop off point. It's catch as catch can at this point. Every woman for herself. Eventually, they arrive home.

After sweeping the place with a two foot broom, the mother starts dinner prep around 6:30. This is their largest meal. They will have several different dishes centering on their staple – ugali. Ugali is made from ground white corn. They pour it into boiling water until you almost can't stir it and then you add another cup or so. It produces a white, bouncy hockey puck, which is then sliced in chunks and put on each plate. Diners then pull off smaller chunks, wad it into a ball and dimple it. They pick up chopped veggies and other items with their thumb and ugali wad, eating without utensils. I try it and wallow in it down to my elbows. *They* leave the table miraculously clean.

Dinner takes two and a half to three hours to prepare. It is dark and the kids have grown quiet. They are hungry but they never complain. They last ate at 1:30 during their break from school when they walk all the way home and then all the way back again. I never hear African kids complain. I once sat with four of them in a car in the hot sun for one and a half hours while the father went to meet with a friend. Not a peep.

Dinner is ready. We light the lantern, hanging it twelve feet from the table. This is a larger home so we can do this. If you get the lamp too close the bugs overwhelm you. We eat in an eerie, shadowy darkness after saying grace for our bounty and blessings, which to these people are many. I'm thankful the strange wailing has stopped for the last several hours so I don't have to think about the families who won't have everyone around the table tonight. But you know something, those families probably still said grace in earnest.

Outside our gate a woman appears with something bundled. It's a child in a blanket. He's only 11 months old and he's very sick. The mother is crying. She has watched him grow worse over the last three days and finally realizes this is malaria. She must get to the hospital and we have the only car that can make the hour journey to Kisii. People are hesitant to go to Kisii hospital, which is filthy and where they often fit three or four people to a single bed, less than four feet across. This woman might have waited too long. An arm extends from the blanket. It's tiny. It trembles and the child is shivering uncontrollably. My eyes well with tears and I say to Christopher, "You've got to help her." The baby now needs a blood transfusion if it hopes to survive.

Christopher drives off with the precious load as I am told about this woman. This is her third child out of wedlock since her husband died. She will never be able to care for all of them and village sympathy will not close the gap. "She brought this on herself," they will say. But what about the kids?

At 9:30 the dishes are stacked. It's too dark to wash them. We'll do that tomorrow. It will take a long time because some of the dishes caramelized under the imprecise heat of the jiko. No non-stick pans here. Once the table is cleared, we head to the chairs where we read Bible passages and sing by fading lantern light. Then we all move to our beds and try to sleep while the room cools from 85 degrees down to 50 over the course of several hours.

No one complains about the heat. They need their energy and they need their sleep. Tonight they sleep on full stomachs. God be praised.

Tomorrow's schedule will be almost identical to today's. There is no leisure. There are no televisions or long phone calls to friends. It's a hard life by Western standards. It's a hard life by African standards.

Around 11:30 PM I drift off. Asleep in the heat of Kenya. I will be awake in less than five hours to start the day again, God willing. I no longer listen for mosquitoes. I need my sleep to digest this large meal, this long day, this Africa.

Chapter Five
Dr. Mzungu

One morning I went with a "cousin" of Christopher's to perform flow rate measurements on the river running through Kodera. He did not speak much English which was okay with me, since measuring a river for true flow rate was silent tedium as you try to exclude back-eddy measurements and other false readings. There wasn't much talking needed but I would have to find several good spots to measure and having some companionship was certainly pleasant enough.

The drawback to a companion with weak English skills is his inability to fend off other people with weak English skills and soon they were arriving in greater numbers. They gathered and talked among themselves for a while but soon they were making suggestions while I waded about as to where I should be placing the tape measure to get the best fix on cubic feet per minute (CFM). Their sense of CFM measurements was different than mine and they wanted to set me right. They also pointed out individually, all of them, one by one and repeatedly that the water was higher at non-drought times. I nodded in agreement but I was obviously not getting it.

I tried as best I could to explain the benefit of knowing the slowest flow time of the year for determining the maximum amount of electrical output at the minimal time. This was met with nods which by now I knew meant, "I have no idea what you are saying, Mzungu, but I'm sure you'll say a word I recognize any time now." Some who possessed better English would repeat with a puzzled look on their face, the gist of my last dependent clause, "Thus, you want to know most when it is least?" They would look around at their fellow villagers with a what- the-__ expression on their face.

So I tried it in Africanized English: Nid tu no wahn water ees vedee wik so no haoo mutch elektreesihtih wahn bahdest. Which is to say, "Need to know when water is very weak so know how much electricity when baddest???" (Now that I replay that translation I admit

I'm confused myself). To this explanation they would say to one another, "I wish I spoke better English because I need to tell him the river is higher at other times of the year." They viewed me as something between an eccentric scientist and a lost soul.

By the way, I did know the Luo word for water. It is "pi" pronounced pee. I just can't bring myself to say it when I am talking about something I am wading in.

At least six different times, one of the villagers would select a spot on the river that he felt should be measured. I found it saved time to just go ahead and measure. There was considerable satisfaction and pride when I would announce the distance on the tape. I would say it in English and Swahili. Counting in Swahili, especially in the higher numbers is essentially Arabic. Since I know how to read and write in Arabic, I felt comfortable. At each pronouncement of distance, there was a response from all the bystanders. An "aaaah" wave would pass through the crowd. There appeared to be some degree of status gained by the people who picked a wider spot and subsequently a higher number. I heard the guy that picked 40 feet qualified for a new wife.

There were three interruptions in one spot from cattle being driven into the river to drink. I don't think the guys that surveyed for Hoover Dam had to put up with this. Each time I would sit on the bank for twenty to thirty minutes. Finally, I decided I had enough to plot CFM and I hiked up the hill through the cornfields, a silent coterie of eight or nine villagers following me single file.

As I came up to the main pathway, I looked off in the distance and saw a young girl standing with her side turned to me. She had a hugely distended stomach. I knew what that was likely to be, so I approached for a closer look. When I got near, her mother approached and observed as I examined the child's head. I was fortunate that in my journey up the hill I picked up one individual who was strong in both Luo and English. The mother knew no English. I turned to the translator.

"Ask her if the little girl's hair has had any red color in it in the last year." I needed to know this to eliminate the possibility of kwashiorkor, the disease caused by insufficient protein in the diet. It is rare outside of Africa but all too common among the poor in remote villages. He exchanged a few words with her.

"No. Her hair hasn't changed color, ever."

"Then tell her that her daughter has intestinal worms and that is why her stomach is sticking out so far." With words and gestures he passed on the message. I continued. "Ask her if I can see her other children."

As we walked the 100 yards or so to her hut, I noticed the mother had a bit larger stomach than I was used to seeing on non-pregnant women. I made a note to myself to follow up on that fact. When we got to the hut there were children playing in the yard. She called them over. Three of the four had huge stomachs with the belly button sticking out three quarters of an inch. "Every one of your kids has worms," I said. "Are these all your kids? Do you have any others? Any babies?"

I was invited into her dark little hut. There, reclining on a cot was Lisa, a three year old girl in a ragged blue dress. She sat up slightly when the mother, the translator and I entered. Her stomach was huge. She seemed listless. I asked if we could take her outside.

Once outside, I looked at her eyes and ears in addition to noting her thickly runny nose. I pointed to the flowing nose. "How long has this been going on?" She had been sick for about a month, maybe a little longer. I tapped her lungs. Solid with fluid. "Can you ask Lisa to stick out her tongue?"

A few words later and the pale coated tongue was out. Her gums were pale. Her eyes were steamy. She coughed thick and deep. I turned to the young man translating for me. "Don't translate, okay?" He nodded in all seriousness. I continued. "This little girl is dying. She's got pneumonia and about a dozen other maladies. She's on her way down."

He glanced over at the mother. She knew something was up when he did not translate. "Just tell her that her daughter is very sick."

As he was translating I stood up. "Ask her if any of her other kids have a cough or an earache or any other pains."

One bad earache, one mild earache, no coughs. "Tell her I am going to go into Kisii to get some medicine." Hearing this she asked the translator to come around the side of the house with her. In a minute they came back. I did not understand why she would go around the house since I can't understand Luo anyway.

"She says her back really aches and it hurts when she goes to the bathroom. She thinks it was from an injection she got."

"How long ago did she get the injection?"

"About a year ago."

"This doesn't have anything to do with the injection, I suspect."

I rubbed her lower back. "Down here?" I asked. She nodded. I turned to the translator. "Tell her she has a bladder infection that is now probably a kidney infection. I'll get her started on some medication, too. Tell her to take Lisa back in the house and have her lay down. She needs rest, lots of boiled water and no milk."

I asked if the mother was expecting a baby. She was sure she wasn't. This was important because the parents needed to be wormed too. Worming a pregnant woman is problematic

After he had translated this last directive I told her to stop all milk drinking so the ear infections and mucous could clear up. With this I started to leave but one of the men who had been listening approached and asked if I would come to his hut. "It was on the way," he added. I told him I would go to his hut even if it wasn't on the way.

When we got there I saw no life; no chickens, goats or children. It was all quiet. We entered his ten by ten hut and I was offered a seat on the living room side. We chatted for a few moments then he told me he wanted me to look at his wife and kids. I said to bring them in. He shouted something and from around the other side six human beings emerged. I have no idea how they could all fit back there in a five by ten foot space but here they were; the kids smiling and shy.

They all had worms, a couple had earaches and one was coughing pretty badly. I wrote in my little book I had brought along for river measurements. I headed out with the same set of directions being imparted.

As I walked back home, a man trotted after me who had briefly seen me look over little Lisa – the one dying of pneumonia. I noticed he was listening very carefully. It turned out he was here visiting family in the village. This was his home village but he worked as a policeman in Nairobi. He asked if I would come look at one other family.

"Relatives?" I asked.

"No, but I think they have some of the same problems," he responded calmly. His name was Thomas and his English was excellent. His sense of compassion was even better. We went together to this third home; the most run down of all. The children were absolutely filthy; their shredded clothes hung off them in tatters and loops. I was invited inside to look them over. The whole family lined up opposite where I was seated. Same answer. Worms.

I went through the usual pain, itching and cough questions. I gave the same instructions and explained I would get worm medicine for everyone and something for the painful ear but not the mild ear infection. No milk. Wash your hands. Blah blah blah. A surge of discouragement swept over me as I looked through the doorway and across the yard at another half dozen kids. All wormy. This was an epidemic. I asked them to join me in prayer. They bowed as Thomas translated. It wasn't making a real specific prayer about the family as much as I just needed to talk to God. This was starting to look like it was way bigger than me.

I started to stand up and leave when I glanced down at the nine year old girl's leg. From the middle of her shin down to the top of her ankle it looked like she had a coating of tar. As I asked about this, I saw the little two and half year old hold his stomach with both hands. I turned to his father. "Is he saying anything about pain in his stomach?"

Pain was not too common with worms. The father simply stared back without answering. So I stood up to walk toward the child.

The child had had his fill. It was scary enough having this strange Mzungu in his home, the first white person he had ever seen, but now I was walking right toward him. He bolted. His screams filled the yard as he zigzagged in every direction. After a while we all laughed. The screaming went on for two full minutes as I continued where I left off with the little girl. Her name was Sarah.

"What is that?" I asked.

"The witch doctor put a root medicine on her leg. It was sick."

"What kind of root?"

Shrugs.

"What did it look like before the witch doctor put that on?" They explained what the leg looked like but it was the least coherent and most contradictory explanation between two parents. I held up my hands to stop them. "I'm going to Kisii to get some medicine. Please, remove the tar and I will look at it when I get back."

I walked home in the hot sun wondering what I had gotten myself into. But I knew that if I did not intervene, a couple of those kids would be dead. We made the long rough and bumpy ride into Kisii and once there I went to the first pharmacist I could find. They call them Chemists in Kenya and I found a great one.

I took out my list of cases and after we worked through the worming count, I was on to the list of other problems. When I came to the pneumonia case he tried to give me a medication that kills bacteria in a wet tissue environment. It was the Kenyan equivalent of erythromycin. I told him I did not think I was going after a primary pneumococcus infection. My theory, which would become very important for the whole village if it was correct, was that the worms weaken the children and they become exposed to other bacteria that would normally not be a threat. I felt she had pneumonia from one of the secondary bugs such as hemophilus or mycoplasma, which have odd replication patterns. These both take a long time to treat.

Here's the problem as I weighed it then: if I treat Lisa for pneumococcus and I'm wrong, it's too late and she will probably die. But, on the other hand, pneumococcus lets you know pretty quickly if the medication is working. However, if I treat her for a secondary pneumonia, which takes at least ten days, and I'm wrong, she will probably die. The third alternative was to get her to Kisii hospital where they could guess, just as I was doing, while having her lay in one filthy bed with several other children. Her parents rejected all my suggestions involving Kisii Hospital. It was Genesis 41:16 time.

When I got back there was still some daylight so I trotted down to the huts of the various families. I went to Lisa, the pneumonia victim first. I had found my interpreter gnawing sugar cane under a papaya tree and he just seemed too peaceful to leave there. He gladly came along and explained to the family the procedure for each medication. We left and went to Peter's house in the ten by ten. Medicine in; worms on their way out. Pills for ear infection and a cough. Thirty minutes of light left and we were off to the final home.

There we went through the procedure for worming and I felt pretty good until I looked over at Sarah the little girl with leg "tar" as she entered the hut. Her leg was still tar-covered. I turned to the father.

"I thought I told you to get that stuff off Sarah's leg."

"We did."

I looked again and squinted in confusion. "Let's get out in the light." I maneuvered her to get the best light. The mother ran to where I was and gave me a little carved stool to sit on. I examined the leg more closely. It was rotting. Little Sarah had gangrene. I washed it with hydrogen peroxide and put some antibiotic ointment on it. I was under-medicating it significantly – shooting BBs at a Sherman Tank.

That night we drove back to Kisii and got there just before the Chemist closed his shop. I got some very strong antibiotic ointment, a steroid cream and some pills to be taken internally to treat Clostridium, the gangrene bacterium, from the inside out. I felt much better armed.

By lantern light we all sat silently in the front yard as I took the hydrogen peroxide and a cotton cloth I had boiled and I rubbed all her rotten skin off, breaking open the pockets of Clostridium. The cleansing was by any measure cruel. Sarah took it amazingly well. The parents sat in silent horror. One of the other people had just explained to them what gangrene meant. They had seen the amputees in their village and in other villages who had let a simple infection take a leg. This was suddenly very serious and I knew they were hating themselves for trusting the witch doctor. They had gone to him when it began to rot. What were their alternatives?

I put Sarah on a regimen of antibiotic pills twice a day and anti-biotic creams twice a day. I would introduce steroids in a couple of days when I returned from Kisumu. In the meantime, the parents had the ball. In truth, I trusted these people. They were serious. The dad openly cared about his children, which is a rare sight among African fathers. He listened to my words and repeated them as I spoke them and then gave me a complete recap just before I left his yard. I nodded in concurrence and patted him on the shoulder. I added a prescription for prayer and he nodded back affirmatively.

As I walked back home I thought about this father and his threatened daughter. I had seen them talking as I passed beyond the perimeter of their yard, their long thin profiles silhouetted in the light of the lantern, still sitting where I left it. He was taking her through the prescribed regimen and she was nodding periodically. I had to think his attachment had to do with character. Sarah had showed a ton of it. And so had he.

When I got home I was informed that Peter wanted to see me. He had the ten by ten foot hut with the six people in one half, in need of treatment. It turned out he was very grateful and wanted to do me a favor. He knew that white people liked to see monkeys. How he knew this, I did not know because I was not aware of this fact myself. I was invited to meet him at 4:00 PM the following day to tour a small clump of forest and possibly see the resident troupe of monkeys.

The next day, I came home in the early afternoon, prior to my appointment with Peter. I was eating a pineapple a woman had given me, when I sensed I was not alone. I peered into the dark sleeping area and saw a thin body move.

"Flo?" I called quietly.

"Yes." She answered in her sweet little voice. Flo was a tall twelve year old girl who had the most delicate frame and tiny little head. Her voice was so soft it was almost inaudible at times. She had moved in with Christopher's family last year when both of her parents died of AIDS within months of one another.

"What are you doing home?"

"I have a headache."

"Did you take anything for it?"

"They gave me something at break."

"When was that?"

"10 AM."

I decided she was dehydrated. A safe guess in Africa since no one drinks enough water. I suppose if every American had to scoop water out of a ditch and boil it, we might get behind on fluids as well. I gave her one of my 1.5 liter bottles of purified water and made her drink half of it before I handed her four Ibuprofen and then made her drink some more. Her assignment by the end of the afternoon was to finish all 1.5 liters and start on a new bottle.

"Is it possible you're having a recurrence of malaria?"

"I think so. They usually go to Kisii and get me a pill when that happens."

"Let's see what the water does first."

I had a theory that the lack of normal hydration and body fluid balance when malaria flares up is part of what makes people feel lousy. Since no one was around to get Flo some medicine, this would be my little, statistically invalid experiment with Flo serving as my sample population.

By evening she was all smiles. She was asking me for another bottle of water. I had created a monster. Over the course of the next several weeks of my stay, I would expend significant effort trying to keep bottles of water available; first for Flo and then for the other children. They had found the exhilaration of being hydrated. I had discovered this fact in college and after graduation when I worked as a waiter in the evening and a house painter during the day. A quart of room temperature water was life-giving.

So take it from Dr. Mzungu, most Africans are dehydrated. I have converted many Americans on this subject and increasing numbers are getting super-hydrated – especially in the morning when I recommend a quart of very warm water, first thing. When Africa solves its water problem, with more abundant *clean* water, mortality and morbidity will be halved or better. Today, I was just dealing with Flo. And she felt great.

|||||||||||||||||||||

At four o'clock, I met in the road with Peter and two other men to go look at monkeys. They had dressed up a bit in freshly ironed shirts and hard shoes, including Peter who was very poor. It appears I was developing an elevated status as time progressed.

We trooped off toward the forest. The men insisted I lead, which was honoring and all except for the fact that I had no idea where I was going. I now knew how the African cattle felt. I always thought they could reduce the amount of cattle beating done while driving the herd by about ninety nine percent if they walked out in front to set the pace and direction. Just a theory.

We toured the forest, ate unripe guavas (the ripe ones are full of bugs) and actually saw monkeys. We also saw birds of all kinds and they gave me the Luo names for them. My favorite was the nga nga. When I asked why it was called a nga nga, the bird, on cue hollered nga nga in a smart allecky voice. Nuff said.

On our way out of the forest, they pointed to a small, dug up area with strange little tree-like plants growing in it. This was where a witch doctor had been digging up medicinal roots. Despite my only experience to date with the gangrenous leg, I did not necessarily think ill of witch doctors. Western medicine owed much to the work of the third world shaman and half of our modern pharmaceuticals are still plant-based. So I asked to meet him. They all decided that would not be a good idea.

Later, I mentioned to Christopher the brief conversation about meeting the witch doctor. He agreed it was best that I not meet the witch doctor. No one ever told me why. When I asked someone he would just think about it for a few moments and kind of shrug and tilt his head and that was the end of the discussion. My horribly inquisitive nature won't allow this and next time I'm in the neighborhood I will be looking the guy up. Curiosity killed the cat. But I'm not sure what it will do to the Mzungu.

Chapter Six
The Road to Kisumu

I was looking forward to going to Kisumu. Located on the northern tip of Lake Victoria, Kisumu is Kenya's third largest city and the metropolis of the Luo speaking people. Cities are ranked by population. Kisumu is populous but the sense of bigness isn't there. It is a sprawling town. Nothing city about it. It is dusty and dirty and I really wanted to see it.

We were to leave at 7:30 in the morning in order to make our 10:00AM with the IDCCS Director. At about 8 o'clock some people strolled into the yard whom I did not recognize and they made their way to the car. The first was a well dressed woman in her late 20's. She shook my hand and climbed into the back seat. I guessed we were having a traveling companion. In the corner of the yard, moving slowly was a young man leading an elderly woman by the hand. She was doubled over and clutching her abdomen. When they finally reached our car, the young man helped her to climb in and then he ran off. I guessed we were having two traveling companions.

It turned out the young woman needed to be dropped off at a small town half way to Kisumu. She was just visiting Kodera. It was revealed later that she had been Kenya's top 800 meter runner and was Olympics bound. Personal issues arose and she faded back into the stark countryside never to be heard of publicly again.

The elderly woman had stomach cancer. She was going to Kisumu to get additional radiation treatment. She was shivering even though the morning sun had already warmed the air to 80 degrees and it was now only 8:30. I took off the nice new sweater I had bought in Nairobi and handed it to her. She took it and put it on without saying a word. I had a strange feeling I was not going to see that sweater again.

Finally we headed for Kisumu. Less than a mile down the road we pulled off and waited in the shade of a tree for twenty minutes. Eventually, a man who had not bathed in a couple of leap years hopped in the back seat next to the women. The stench was overwhelming. I looked around to see if everyone else was equally horrified. Nobody blinked. In fact they engaged in friendly conversation immediately. I was aghast. Quickly, I rolled down my window and rudely stuck my head out and, with nostrils enlarged to the size of quarters, pumped my diaphragm muscles without decorum.

I leaned back inside, holding my breath as I checked to see if everyone was okay. They were still just chatting. I asked Christopher where we were taking our fragrant friend and was dismayed to learn he was escorting the old woman to Kisumu Regional Hospital. We would also be giving him a ride back. This was going to be a long ride. Fortunately, I would soon find something that would take my mind off this new threat to Earth's fragile atmosphere: the road to Kisumu.

To say Kenyan roads are bad is tantamount to saying Hitler was un-neighborly. Your speed on the Kisumu highway will vary from 120 kilometers to 0 to 50 and back to 120 kilometers – all in the same mile. Potholes and ditches and humps and cracks. Perhaps one of the reasons Kisumu is so populous was that the people who survived the drive to the city were unwilling ever to leave again by the same route. I thought the old woman was going to fail the road test portion of her therapy. I thought I was next.

We dropped the track star off in the middle of absolutely nowhere. I watched as she climbed into an already full matatu and then watched as four more people were stuffed in behind her. I wonder if she ever thought about where all that wonderful running, racing and training had brought her in life. I could barely make out which of the dark heads was hers inside the dark cab of the matatu that belched smoke and pulled off toward the dusty treeless horizon.

We eventually made it to Kisumu where we dropped off the elderly lady and her eye-watering companion at the largest hospital in western Kenya. We hurried to IDCCS headquarters and had a quick meeting because, being one and a half hours late, we had messed up a pretty tight schedule. It turned out they had scheduled all the village elders in the town of Jera, 120 km to the north, to meet with us. A driver in a four-wheel drive Toyota expanded cab pick up truck was waiting. We climbed in and raced north to Jera.

We soon found out why we were taking the Toyota. The Peugeot would not have survived the roads. They were worse by far than the roads we had come in on. A quarter of the time we drove on the shoulder because it was smoother than the shelled concrete. In some places the roads were just gone.

They called these Moi highways, in honor of the former president whose system of graft diverted money slated for highways, medicine and housing into the pockets of his unbelievably greedy friends. I would label them frantically greedy. Toward the end, they did not even make an attempt to fake that they were using the money as allocated. In the old days, they would at least spray tar over the road, potholes and all. In the last couple of years they snatched every dime. Now my teeth were rattling and my head was slapping against the side of the cab as we rocked and roiled toward Jera – all because men of greed had completely befouled their own country. The amazing thing was the fact that the former officials still lived there; surrounded by the squalor they had created. They didn't even have the decency to move to nicer digs and enjoy the fruits of their despoiling.

North of the Equator the impossible happened: the roads got worse. I have now been freed of all those extraneous ligaments and tendons which bound my neck bones to my back and shoulders. I felt like a bobble-head doll. The pivot point on my neck is now two vertebrae lower. These weren't potholes. These were excavations. There were transecting ditches, sometimes nine inches deep. The road was littered with rocks (boulders), car parts, a half a bicycle (the other half is on some car's grill going in the other direction), a goat carcass, glass everywhere and one or two unsecured but intact spinal columns proving you gotta wear your seatbelt.

Once the driver looked at his watch and decided we were running late – a phenomenon I considered heretofore not possible in Kenya. In fact, there is no equivalent to the English word "late" in any of the African dialects I am familiar with. In any event, something he saw on his watch caused him to suddenly abandon the paved road and take to the dirt shoulders and walkways. He did this for miles at a time, scattering goats, donkeys and Kenyans. The goats scattered fastest followed by Kenyans and then donkeys. I was personally rooting for the Kenyans to be quickest to spring but everyone in the car agreed, with refreshing objectivity I might add, that the goats were quicker than the Kenyans. My polite urgings to slow down as we approached humans seemed to spur our driver to press the pedal harder. So on behalf of the Kenyans, et al, I shut up.

We finally pulled off the highway and navigated eight miles of dirt roads and rock outcroppings that could not have been negotiated in the Peugeot. We arrived at the Jera clinic - a small, open air, three-room shelter that was a life-saving oasis in the middle of a desperately poor village in Luo country. It was staffed by three women: a volunteer, a local nurse and a public health nurse on loan from the Ministry of Health. They were wonderfully dedicated people; treating many of the same ailments I was treating in Kodera: pneumonia, worms, leg ulcers and gangrene. We compared notes like two cooks sharing and improving on favorite recipes.

"Oh, I always assume Clostridium is flourishing with gangrene, even before I rule out diabetes."

"Now, that's a good idea. I like to shake a little gramacin into those two-inch leg ulcers once the hydrogen peroxide foam has subsided. It's a good thing."

"I just assume I'm going to treat scabies twice but that's just me."

When we arrived at the Anglican Church building, the village elders rose politely and stood in silence as we were seated in the chairs of honor next to the podium. We were over an hour late and yet no one said a word. I apologized profusely. They just smiled and began their program describing how they had used community planning to begin transforming their village. They had also dealt with worms. While they were able to catch it in a far earlier stage than we were experiencing in Kodera, it was encouraging to know they had finally gotten it under control.

After the pastor gave his little talk on how the church had participated, he went to sit down but I asked him to wait. I wanted to know if the Luo in Jera were engaging in the same unchristian-like practices as elsewhere: wife beating, plural marriages, drinking to excess and wife-inheritance practices. He admitted they were but gave a tremendously bold talk on how he was confronting it. This was a courageous man, as uncompromising in dealing with pagan infiltration as the Apostle Paul. I told him I was honored to meet him.

We toured pineapple mini-plantations, irrigated cassava patches and a newly tapped well. Then we headed back to Kisumu where we picked up the old lady's escort but not the old lady. It turned out she was taking a turn for the worse. It was 7 PM and getting dark. It was time to head back onto the Kisumu highway.

The night drive had a mixture of scariness like bad airplane turbulence combined with the eeriness of the jungle scenes in *Apocalypse Now*. I was no longer focused on the moonscape roughness of the road. Merely being on this highway after dark would prove to be far more disturbing. For more than 40 miles we passed one bike or pedestrian after another. Spirits flickered in our lights as they seemed to emerge from nowhere along the side of the road. High speed, undivided highways were scary enough. This was deadly.

A lane in one direction would hold a bike rider, a car and often the edge of an oncoming truck. And they kept coming and coming and coming. We overtook one bike after another. It felt surreal and darkly ethereal, like we were pulling them out of the mists in front of us. No lights on these bikes. No reflectors. The riders wore dark clothing and carried large dark loads. Someone was going to get killed as happened every night in Kenya, by the dozens.

Inches meant life or death. The bicyclists had to be terrified too, with their backs turned to oncoming vehicles, often a child or two on the rear fender. They sometimes rode for ten or twenty miles or more to get home from jobs and school. It was 8:30 at night and many were still far from home and supper, if they made it.

Music by the *Doors* played in my mind as each apparition emerged and came at us.

Conditions were further exacerbated by the fact that no one would dim their high beams. If you do, you'll be the only one doing so. With each oncoming car, you are temporarily blinded for up to 300 yards. Bicyclists and pedestrians are most vulnerable then. The most haunting looks were on the faces of the fathers as they pedaled home with their children clinging to them.

It had to happen. When we were almost to the turnoff at Kisii we rounded a bend and saw another apocalyptic scene. A bus had pulled over and hundreds of people lined the road. Lights came from everywhere as though a performance were underway. Several people were gathered around the body of a woman in her twenties, lying off to the side. People were waving for each car to stop and somehow help but there were already too many vehicles there now. Other people, perhaps thirty or more of them, were breaking branches and throwing them into the center of the roadway. They don't have road flares or reflective hazard triangles so they throw plants in both directions to caution traffic.

We made it home near 10 PM, shaken. Eating at a dimly lit table in a dark, non-electrified dwelling in western Kenya did little to knock the thick pall out of the macabre air that surrounded everything that night. I did not look up as I ate but I sensed a presence in the quiet, moonless night. I wasn't afraid. I had just seen enough to know there was a side of Kenya where evil had free reign.

Chapter Seven
Running in the Land of Runners

Running has a special meaning to Kenyans. As early as the second morning, I had started with a run from my dwelling to Mititi School and back. I did it three times for a total of seven and one half miles. At 6000+ elevation, I was not at full power. Normally, my training runs clip along at about 6:30 per mile but I was at least a minute slower this day. I realized this just as soon as I came off the flats and started up the mile long hill to Mititi. At about the point the modest climb began I came across a group of children walking to school. They all looked at me in amazement and then they waved and smiled. A white person was a rare sight. A running white person in a nation of runners was rarer yet. In fact, it was pretty much unheard of in these parts.

To my gasping horror, one of the children decided to join me. And he was a quick little bugger. He announced his entry into the event with the slapping of cheap plastic sandals. They contrasted loudly with my $80 dollar running shoes. My young partner was about five foot two and probably 105 pounds. He was a terrific runner.

He ran to the cheers of his fellow students who were now present in droves along the way. I had picked an odd time to run if I were seeking solitude. He surged next to me and then started to press. I picked up the pace each time he challenged me. In the distance I saw my psychological opportunity. The path would soon level off and the natural tendency in this kind of road race is to catch a breather after a long hard climb. Despite the fact that he was a good runner and despite the fact that he was acclimated to an altitude that was sapping my strength, he was competing with a fully warmed-up runner who had done interval training for the last few months. He was also starting mid-hill and mid-run and you just can't do that very easily.

He was starting to breathe hard now and his look was more serious. He had an audience of about half his school. When we hit the level the kids were not only cheering, they were applauding. I took off.

Glancing back, I saw a look of complete dismay. Psychologically, he was caught off guard. In a split second, I reduced my pace without making it clear I was giving him a break. He regained his spot near my side. His eyes brightened and the smile started to reappear.

We rounded the last bend and I saw the gatepost entrance to the large field that was in front of the school. That was my turnaround point and his point of departure. As we approached the gate I slowed so he could see I was not going in. As he came along side, I patted him on the shoulders and he gave me a little rub in the small of my back. As I turned around to head back home, I saw him being mobbed by boys and girls who were animated and laughing. He was a little hero.

Later that night I was approached by the high school boy who was living with us. "Charles, I would like to run with you. When can we run?" He was dead serious. This was a *must do* activity.

"Calvince, how did you know I was a runner?"

"It was all over school that a white man ran with one of the students. I want to run with you." I agreed but I told him that since I had run twice that day, I was going to give myself at least a day of rest so he would have to be patient. Besides, my second seven mile run had been at 2 PM and the heat had cooked my innards thoroughly – an affliction I would shortly come to regret in a country that was not abounding in either Pepto-Bismol or porcelain.

What is interesting is that I had run with an eighth grader who went to a completely different school than Calvince, yet Calvince knew all the details. When you hear about the African drums and how word spreads quickly on the Dark Continent, believe it.

This wasn't jogging. As I continued to run and get stronger and as more serious high school students would join me on the running path, with mixed results, it seemed there was not a single person in the village of 7000 who did not know about the running Mzungu. It was a cause of interest, excitement or concern depending on whom you spoke to.

Each time I went for a run, there were no less than a dozen school children challenging me at any given point. They would fold in with the pack and then peel off to be replaced by another excited, sandal wearing trackster. This went on day after day. Occasionally, a high school boy would join in and it would get serious. No smiles, no looking about at peers. This was a test. Many of them would stick with me all the way to the school entrance, despite my sneaky tricks. How they did this without any training, I don't know, but it greatly added to my own buy-in to the mystique of the Kenyan runner.

I was reminded of what happened a number of years ago when the Swedish Olympic middle distance runners went to Kenya to do altitude training for the Olympics. They showed up at the track and were beaten by dozens of high school kids. How were they going to compete against the best in the world if almost any kid with above average talent could run them off the track, at will? That had to be disheartening.

I can also attest to a twinge of self-doubt as I ran alongside Calvince. His natural gait and the smooth roll of his shoulders was as musical as it was powerful. We completed the first round trip of two and half miles and started back for the second lap. This was normally my speed lap. At times, he would say, "Reduce speed" and I would slow down. Yet something told me he could have handled it. At the end of the second round trip, we came to the quarter mile hill that led to our home and starting point. Just then, Calvince announced a race to the gate. I obliged and he moved out impressively. He beat me by a full twenty yards. He was unaware we had another two and a half miles to go. I completed the last lap by myself. They hadn't seen *all* my sneaky tricks. I will however admit that I could not have kept up with him.

If Calvince were in America, he would be on varsity in any school in the nation and easily on his way to a scholarship. In Kenya, he was just one of thousands. In Kodera, he will never be heard of.

One morning, when my running program first started, I was scooting along at a fair clip. Suddenly, a 12 year old boy burst through a hedge holding a live chicken. He turned and saw me speeding toward him only twenty feet away. His eyes widened and without a pause, he seized the opportunity to become one of the alumni of the

Mzungu runners club. As I passed, he jumped next to me and took off, sandals slapping, chicken tucked snugly under his arm. He did remarkably well for almost a mile and quarter. That is exactly one and a mile and quarter farther than I have run carrying any type of poultry.

A few weeks later, a number of older adults, mostly teachers, were sitting around the table in a serious discussion. It was all in Luo and I couldn't follow much of it. At one point I sensed they were talking about me, so I asked what the subject was. One of them explained that they were assessing the fitness of their youth. If a person such as myself was able to outrun many of the teen age boys, then they needed a fitness program. I felt honored to be the gauge for high school decrepitude.

Chapter Eight
Women

I often tell people that 90 percent of the work done in the villages of Kenya is done by women. I tell this lie to improve my credibility because 95 percent sounds like hyperbole, even though it is the more correct estimate. It's not a secret. Everyone knows it. The men know it. They're just glad they aren't women. The women say almost nothing unless you ask them.

Kenyan women are amazing. They work hard, they are nice, they are intelligent, responsible, committed and they rarely complain. In addition to that, they are strikingly gorgeous, especially in eastern Kenya and Nairobi. There, an artful mix of Somali, Kikuyu, and Coast tribes, has produced an allotment of runway models which has not yet been discovered.

And they dress nicely. For approximately nine US dollars, a woman goes to the tailor, picks out material, is measured and then comes back for a beautifully crafted outfit complete with darts, pleats and matching belt. Often a scarf or hair wrap is cut and edged out of the same material and included with the dress. As a result, women in the larger cities like Nairobi have good sized wardrobes over time. Even village women wear dresses or pleated skirts in their everyday activities.

One lasting picture I have in my mind is that of a woman at a roadside marketplace waiting in the hot sun to sell twenty potatoes she had stacked neatly on a small makeshift table. She stood with her arms at her side, her long hair combed out and down to her shoulders, wearing a gray wool skirt and silk blouse, delicate facial features and large dark eyes, just staring. I looked back several times as we attempted to merge into Nairobi traffic. She never moved; the wooden stare appeared to be a permanent feature.

She was surrounded by junky looking businesses. On her right were tables of car parts being sold by sloppily dressed men gathered in bunches to talk and carry on. To her left was a trash heap smoldering next to a pile of scrap iron, some tomato sellers and a couple of tables of cheap electronics.

It's a haunting notion, but if I drove back today she might still be standing there with that vacant stare, waiting for the day to pass.

As I got to know some of these women, I found them to be sharp minded and clear thinking. They knew the facts but they never seemed to have an axe to grind; at least not the size axe I would have had which would have shamed Paul Bunyan. They simply took care of the things they were forced to deal with every day of every week of every year. Talking to them, they discuss their day and occasionally gaze past me, out over a Kenyan landscape where they see a horizon farther away than I could see and a dirt road that chases the sky forever.

When speaking, their voices are often subdued and always soft. There is a sweetness in these women that is rare elsewhere. It was once said of my wife, "There is nobody that does not like Kristy." She has the same sweetness that takes nothing away from her strength, her toughness even. The Kenyan women were almost uniformly that way. Universally, they are under-appreciated by their mates. In fact, it appeared to be a point of pride in the men to overlook their good fortune to have a wife exuding charm, character and industry.

When I would point out my observations on women's workload to men they would agree, to a man, that it was way out of balance by any scale in the cosmos. However, they had no intention of lifting a finger to move the bubble toward level. Why should they? They inherit land from their fathers while the father is still alive. Women inherit nothing. The men then go get a wife - one to begin with - bring her back home and she does all the work to hold up her end of the deal.

You cannot look at the marriage of two Kenyans as anything romantic. There are no fairy tale fantasies among young Kenyan women. They know marriage to be what it is – a business deal. Two people enter into a partnership to sustain themselves, to survive or in rare cases to thrive. Offspring are produced and the odds of survival are weighed in advance based on their surroundings. Once the odds are calculated, the parents then invest themselves emotionally to a greater or lesser extent. The greatest grief occurs when a child reaches adulthood against the odds and then dies. A younger child is grieved over but not in a lasting fashion. Were it otherwise, Kenya would be a land of emotional cripples.

Fathers are unlikely to become attached to any of their children. Wives are partners. Children are employees whose appearances at birth are proofs of virility. The relationship between fathers and their children is distant and cool. The emotional burden of rearing children is placed on the women. Kenyan kids are smart and they know there is a line between themselves and their fathers. This line begins to fade when the child matures into adulthood. For the safety of the children, the women ensure it is not crossed prior to that.

In the past, men were responsible for hunting, tribal defense and lifting very heavy objects – in that order. Those jobs pretty much disappeared over forty years ago. So now men are between jobs. In the meantime, there's work to be done.

Let's talk about wife beating because no one in Kodera *would* talk about it. In fact, though it is epidemic throughout Kenya, no one really wants to admit it exists, let alone explore the mystery. I call it a mystery just because of the nonsensical aspect of it all. If I were the individual in a partnership who did virtually zero work to hold up my end of the deal, the last thing I would do is beat bloody and broken the sole working partner. That's just bad business.

The typical cycle associated with wife beating does not take place in Kenya due, in part, to the lack of a romantic base. There is cultural support for the institution of knocking your spouse around the mud hut. So the cycle never really gets a good start. Let me describe the typical cycle, as it occurs in America and the West.

In Western culture, a man is angered by something and then focuses his anger on his wife. He beats her. She apologizes. He cools down and then he hits the hard wall of remorse. The wife is then subjected to a period of his maudlin melancholy, in my opinion, the second round of abuse. He then makes promises never to do it again. She then makes promises never to slice the tomatoes into quarters instead of eighths or whatever set him off. Peace prevails, flowers arrive and all is well until she forgets to put the cap on the toothpaste. It's a classic addiction, abuse, remorse cycle.

No such script plays out in Kenya. One afternoon, a man walked into the clearing where I was staying. I had treated him a week earlier for huge leg ulcers that were an inch and a half in diameter and a half inch deep. He had opened them since I treated him and he was back for another round of medication. These sores were gruesome. They had to be painful. I was frustrated he had opened them up so soon after the last treatment. They were never going to heal.

"How did this happen?" I asked as I poured hydrogen peroxide directly into the sores and watched them foam up like warm beer in a cold mug.

He winced and leaned back as he spoke through clenched teeth. "I was plowing. I hit a clump."

I poured gramacin powder into the raw craters. "John, you have two wives. Can't they plow until you get this under control? It will never heal if you don't stay out of the fields."

I explained that I was going to leave them open this time with the new powder. He agreed to let his wives plow and he hobbled out of the yard to wherever he lived. That night I recounted the conversation and when I finished, people shuffled and avoided making eye contact with me. "What's up?" I asked. "What are you guys thinking?"

"You know, John has had those sores for almost ten years."

"Well, we're fixing that, Lord willing. Is that why everyone is fidgeting?"

After another pause, one of the more articulate men volunteered. "His wives cannot plow. He will just be back out there ripping up his legs again."

"Why is that?" I asked.

"Last night he beat his wives so bad, he broke the younger one's hand and the older one had her collar bone broken. There was evidently a lot of screaming and it went on for almost an hour."

When I asked what the men were going to do about it, the meeting more or less broke up as people muttered a few Luo phrases to one another and then went off into the darkness to their huts. I was left standing there trying to plot what *I* could do about it. This had occurred one day before I was to leave for America. I still had to go meet with the Ministry of Health before I left. Running out of time, yet confronted with something that needed to be addressed, I was torn. Eventually, I did what many well intentioned, ultimately useless people do, I put it off. I would confront it when I was back in Kenya. Someday. Later.

The difference I suppose between what we do in the suburbs, besides having thicker walls and more complicated reasons for rationalizing, is that most men have nothing but the greatest abhorrence for striking a woman. With the exception of a handful of the Christians in the village, wife beating was fully tolerated. In fact, it turns out you are expected to beat your wife. Let me explain further.

We were all sitting around discussing the issue of wife beating, due mostly to my persistence in bringing it up. It bothered me so. Most of these were mild mannered, articulate men and a couple of them were Christians. However, I still sensed some hesitation to condemn wife beating outright. Here's how the conversation went.

"Men used to beat their wives all the time. It was considered taboo *not* to beat your wife at least once in the course of your marriage," one of the men in his late thirties divulged.

"Taboo?" I questioned. "How is this practice enforced? What does everyone do when a husband hasn't beaten his wife?

"Well, first of all, everyone knows who beats his wife. It is known. If a man is too soft on his wife he is spoken to by the others. He may say, 'But she has done nothing wrong!' To this they would say, 'Are you telling us that you have a wife that is so much more good than our wives?'"

"Does that work?" I asked. I wanted to know the power of peer pressure in this ingrained custom. Perhaps, if a few influential men were to push back, there was hope for turning things around someday.

"Sometimes. But when a man will not first beat his wife, he is still the same man. She must give him a better reason to be beaten. If he looks and starts to say 'Why did you do this? Or 'Why did you do that?' maybe she will argue or say something that will make it easier for him to beat her."

"So, according to the custom," I continued, "What will happen to the man who fails to beat his wife?"

"Well, there is always the opportunity as long as they are married that he will beat her. But if she should die and he has never beaten her then at her funeral he must walk up and slap her on the bottom." He demonstrated with a healthy swing as he slapped his hands together. He continued, "She is left on a table, lying on her side at the funeral. Once she has been slapped, they put her in the coffin."

"So it's not just a ritual slap, to go through the motions. It's a real hard slap. Is he angry?" I was really struggling to understand this custom and put in an earthly context.

"Maybe he is angry for being embarrassed."

I then asked, after giving it some thought, but evidently not enough, "What happens if the husband dies first and has never beaten his wife?" Rural Africans can look at you in a way that asks, "Are all white men this stupid?" Almost speechless, he held out his hands, palms up, as if to show he had nothing else to offer. Leaning forward, so I could hear his voice go up one quiet octave, "He is dead!"

Perhaps that was the consequence of the taboo.

||||||||||||||||

One case of wife beating did not go as per routine. It turned into husband beating. Remember these are women who at the age of seventy five can hoist a five gallon ceramic pot full of water onto their heads and walk several miles. Here's one villager's story:

"I had to rescue my cousin. I heard him shouting and calling for help so I rushed over to his house and found his wife beating him. When she saw me she held him down and I said, 'Let him go or so help me I will hit you!' She let him go and walked back into the house. My cousin and I met with several men who were very angry. One of them said, 'I will go to your house and I will beat her. She will know she cannot do that and expect it will be all right.'

"So he got up right then and he went to her house and we waited but we did not hear from him. After a while we went to his house. He had been beaten up and he had run.

"Then another man went to her and he was beaten up by her. She knocked him around good and hard. He never touched her.

"Finally, a third man who was very large and like the other two was a known wife beater, said, 'I will crush this terrible woman.' He went to her house and she beat him worst of all."

Now, I'm not real fond of violence but I can't help but smile as I write this in my journal. I nevertheless showed concern and I asked if I could meet her. In a way I admired her.

"Oh, she is gone! Several of us went to her as a group and we said, 'You are very bad. You get out.' And she left the village."

"Where did she go?" I asked.

"Oh, I don't know. When you are put out, you are put out. You must just go. She is gone. That is all I know. She was a terrible person."

The evil of men hurting women morphs and spreads over time. Such is the nature of evil. Evil is not our qualitative assessment from a distance. It's not an adjective. It is an entity. One particularly grizzly event took place in the previous decade. A group of boys from an all-male high school broke into an all female high school and raped approximately 100 of the girls. Of those raped, more than 60 were raped to death. This is unimaginable to every Kenyan who hears a retelling of this horror. But it is what happens when things are so wrong that women are viewed as a means to an end rather than viewing man and wife as one flesh under a sovereign God.

A second incident occurred where boys poured gasoline all over the roof of a girl's school and set it afire killing several of the students inside. This particular incident coming so soon after the prior enormity, caused numbness as much as any other single emotion. Everyone knew it was time to do something. But what? And where to start?

If anyone thinks that the way things have been is a little off but somehow it will all work out, that person could not be more wrong. Bad things always become worse when injustice is institutionalized or rationalized or both. This too is the nature of evil. Failure to enact appropriate safeguards by law and then enforce them by custom perpetuates such institutionalized injustice. The previous government under Moi used injustice as a stepping stone across the river of suffering humanity that is Kenya. The people of Kenya have had enough. The women of Kenya have had more than enough. Unfortunately, the tolerance of evil practices has become almost epidemic. The Kenyans are in a deeper hole than they realize.

There is a drawing, often duplicated that appears throughout offices in Kenya. It shows a creature with a woman's face, a mule's body, and water pipes where front legs should be. She is standing out in a field, hitched to a plow and holding a baby. The caption says something to the effect of "Woman carries a man's burdens, ploughs his fields, acts as a people producing machine and is an effective substitute for water pipes."

This is not far from what I have seen to be true. It deeply disturbs many responsible Africans; not just someone like me who wanders in without knowing the whole story. I may not know the whole story but I do know I don't like this particular chapter.

A little story, while we're on the subject of women, directly from my journal.

I had purchased some red grapes when I was in Kisumu and I brought a few back to Kodera. The woman of the house came walking in from the kitchen holding one grape away from her as if she had just found a mummified rodent in the bread drawer. She wanted to know what it was. I told her it was a grape. She still wanted to know what it was.

"Is it like a plum?" she asked.

"Well, it doesn't have a pit and it tastes different."

"So, no seed?"

"It has little seeds."

"More than one?" she asked with growing doubt. This sounded worse than a plum.

"Yes, but they are tiny." It then struck me how to turn this conversation around. "You know what a raisin is, don't you?"

"Raisin? No."

Rats.

You might think of grapes as little plums with smaller seeds that you can swallow."

"OK." She left, still holding it away from herself and put it back in the bag.

I believe it will be important for me to eat several grapes in the course of the next week and even more important that I don't die if I hope to win a convert.

Author's Note: I eventually ate all the grapes myself.

Chapter Nine
Dead Zebra

After my second drive to Kisumu and an eight hour jarring return, I was relaxing with a group of village men as the evening turned from dusk to dark. The sky was a mixture of pinks and purples, oranges and grays. It put all of us to silence as we watched to see how God would lay out the last strokes of this, another caducous masterpiece, as stirring as it was unenduring. Yet it remains in my mind to this day along with those close-cropped black profiles that were positioned between me and the show on the horizon.

As grays dominated and then turned to the ashen char of a celestial fire-pit, I broke the silence. "I saw a dead zebra lying in the highway with its tongue hanging out of its mouth. It was at least twenty inches long. And I thought to myself, 'Now that's something you don't see everyday.'"

"A twenty inch tongue?"

"No. A dead zebra. They don't have zebras where I come from."

"They are being crowded out by civilization here also. Soon it will be like America – no more zebras." They all nodded in solemn agreement.

"Actually, there never were zebras."

"Are there no grasslands?"

"There's lots of grass."

They spoke among themselves and then offered this possibility: "Maybe it's the wrong kind of grass. You know the wildebeest eats one part of the grass after the zebra eats the tops. Maybe if there is different grass…"

"There never were zebras. Ever."

They simply did not believe me. Here, zebras are like deer in America. They're everywhere. They also believed the disappearance of zebras was a recent event, occurring some time in the last couple of years.

"So you never saw a zebra before you came here?" One of them asked me.

"Yes. In a zoo."

They looked at one another and nodded in a knowing way and then they looked at me as if to say, "There are zebras, you just don't know where to look."

Chapter Ten
Masai Mara

A break was sorely needed. Only four hours drive away was the upper end of the great Serengeti reserve, stretching from deep in Tanzania and across the border into Kenya. It is called Masai Mara. It's where the wildebeest migrate to. This annual phenomenon is recorded on those African documentaries showing wildebeest crossing a river full of crocodiles, where they are grabbed, rolled and drowned.

I sometimes wonder if I'm alone in thinking that all this predation is not a *natural* thing. Nature was never intended to be "red in tooth and claw" (read Gen 1:30). I can't and won't intellectualize the *beauty* of a gazelle being taken down or the waters turning scarlet as wildebeest are flipped about in terror. Someday the lion *will* lie down with lamb and "eat straw like the ox" (Isa 65:25). Crocs will get algae.

It was drought time when we arrived. No wildebeest scenes to threaten my delicate sensibilities. The wildebeest are in Tanzania. Drought time has a wholly different, genuinely African screenplay.

Kichwa Tembo is a resort in the trees lining the great Masai Mara savannah. As you drive in off a dirt road, just about a mile before you arrive at Kichwa Tembo, you get a view from the hills all the way to the curve of the earth. Dotting the grasslands are acacia trees with their spreading flat tops. This view of the territory is how the Masai Mara got its name. (Mara means dots). I love acacia trees. An acacia tree surrounded by golden dried savannah grass is my picture of Africa from childhood. Add a few elephants and some giraffes and I'm happy.

Between the drought times and the pending conflict between the US led coalition and Iraq, the tourist population was almost non-existent. I had the place all to myself at times. I came with Christopher from the village. As a native he was actually rare for having seen Masai Mara before. Without access to car, it is an unattainable goal for most rural Kenyans.

When we checked in, the receptionist wanted to charge us both 8200 Kenya Schillings (about $114 US). This included all meals and the safari rides that went out three times a day. This wouldn't be too bad in the US or Europe but at the low point in the tourist season it was a bit high. Add to this the fact I was paying for both Christopher and myself, and it was time to negotiate.

I asked if there was a "missionary" rate and the receptionist immediately went to get the manager. The manager, Edward, then told me the price all over again. I told him that it seemed like a fair price to me for my stay but the only reason my friend was along was to help *me* -not to sight see. I felt I was paying twice.

He held firm.

So what was my bargaining position? Here I was in Masai country, hundreds of kilometers from any other accommodation. I was here to see the wildlife of the Serengeti. It's not as though I could threaten to go somewhere else or shame him with the good prices just 500 kilometers down the cratered road in Tanzania. My African friend had argued with African logic but to no avail. There was only one thing left to convince steely-eyed Edward, to give me a break.

"Edward, I need you to help me get a better price."

"On what basis do I give you a discount?"

"I would like a discount for my interpreter."

"This man is your interpreter?" he asked in mild surprise, pointing to Christopher.

"Yes."

"Is he teaching you a language?" (His definition of "interpreter").

"In fact he is," I responded without blinking.

"And what language is that?"

"English. How am I doing so far?"

That broke the stalemate. With a loud laugh he lowered the price to 3200 shillings per night for my "interpreter" Christopher. I later heard him tell and retell the story to others. I was treated extremely well at Kichwa Tembo.

Kichwa Tembo is Swahili for Elephant's Head (head (of) elephant). There is a massive skull of an elephant at the African village-like entrance to the hotel. The lodge is run by an ecotourism firm out of South Africa. It is a very good place to stay. The rooms are large tents with two beds, dressers, zipper windows, and a large stone bathroom with a natural stone shower. It was my first shower in weeks – a real change from the rag and bucket-of-cold-water showers I had been taking.

Our first safari was in an open Land Rover. We saw just about everything Africa has to offer except wildebeest and crocodiles. The grass is shoulder height to a lion, in most places, and that is where the driver focused most of his efforts. Now here is where the rest of humanity and I depart, evidently. Everyone wants to see a lion or two. Or twenty. And they want to see them every time they go out. Drivers call to one another via radio and converge if one driver spots a lion.

Here's the breaking news: Lions are large, unmarked, mostly recumbent cats. Once every two or three days they kill some beautiful mother antelope or a perky little warthog mama. They tackle their breathless pray after a short, desperate run, where the lions had a head start, and then they suffocate their prey. The females do the hunting and the males, if present, eat first. There is nothing admirable about lions. In fact, one-on-one, they regularly get a good whoopin' from the huge buffalo that roam the Serengeti. The rangers will tell you they fear the buffalo and hippos far more than they fear the lions. Our guide said, "If you are ever out in the wild and you get caught between a buffalo and a lion, run toward the lion."

I personally would prefer to curl into a moist little ball, the way you're told to do for grizzly bears in Montana. I'm not running at anything with either claws or a half-ton rack of horns. I simply nodded like a good tourist at his suggestion and continued to stare at the sleeping, tan, unmarked cat. It slept magnificently, better than on TV. Inhale, pause, exhale, long pause….

Now, giraffes on the other hand *are* interesting. They have two little antennae between their ears, which have undoubtedly earned many a wordy speculator his PhD. One of the people on the Land Rover explained that these appendages dissipate heat. Let's see… two inch nibs on a 17 foot, 8,000 pound body mass. If they could dissipate enough heat to make a difference they would be glowing red hot and setting the acacias on fire. I think they are God's party trick to see which blowhard can come up with the best wrong reason and still keep a straight face. Giraffe antennae and warthog tails confirm there is a God and He has a great sense of humor.

After the giraffes moved off, we found to my delirious excitement, a lioness walking down the road with the insouciance of an American high school girl on her way to math class. We followed at a distance of only three or four paces even though we were in a completely open vehicle. This led to some agitation on the part of most of the passengers. I was never afraid. This could have been due to my stoic English heritage and upbringing or possibly it was due to the fact that between me and the lion were two large, fleshy women that might as well have had "Purina Lion Chow" stamped on their foreheads.

My third layer of reassurance came when a warthog darted across the road twenty yards in front of the lioness. She didn't even turn her head. When it finally turned off the road to lie down and finish digesting its little, brown-eyed baby antelope, we turned and headed for leopard country.

As evening fell and we drove back, we saw many hyenas and a couple of jackals. We also watched a leopard at close range munch on gazelle d'jour. Parked just 12 feet below it in our Land Rover, it was the African equivalent of a drive-in movie. It had been a great safari.

That night I lay in my bed reading and listening to the bizarre noises of the African plain. At about 11:30, I turned out my light and rolled over to go to sleep. In the silence I heard what sounded like an endless procession of people returning from the main lodge as they trod along the gravel path. After about five minutes it became irritating. Then I recalled there was no gravel path.

I got up out of bed and looked out to the front tent path. There, just four feet outside my porch, was a group of warthogs, kneeling on their front legs the way warthogs do, eating the grass. They mow it. Each bite is a precise rip of grass. There was my gravel path sound. It was warthogs. I lay back down and thought to myself, "When was the last time I was kept awake by warthogs mowing the lawn?" Bliss.

The next morning we went to a different sector of the reserve. This time we saw elephants and hippos. These are the chunky boys of the Serengeti. The hippos were in a pond of lily pads. When we first drove up I saw nothing but a breeding area for mosquitoes. Within a few moments, round heads and nostrils poked up through the plants and then whole, bulbous swamp-piggies of enormous girth and mouth appeared. Of all the African animals, hippos kill the most humans every year, followed by crocodiles. This is true unless of course you count machete-wielding, human, male, genocidal revolutionaries or the equally deadly matatu drivers.

Mid-morning, the driver took me to a Masai village. We sat inside of one of their bleak, flat-topped little huts in an enclosed compound and spoke with the chief at length. When we first arrived, a line of women sang us a welcoming song. It was long and lovely. Somewhere between the eighth and ninth chorus, I asked the chief if I could stand amid the singers to get my picture taken.

Now, it's important to point out that we were also standing where the cattle were kept the prior evening. Whereas in America one fly can ruin a dinner party and concomitantly your social standing, in Africa there appears to be an entirely different tolerance level. They appear to judge by weight. At somewhere between three and four kilos of manure flies, they made an imperceptible shake of the head and all of the flies from the entire chorus line headed for the Mzungu – me. Multiply: six times four kilos of manure flies...

While the chief feigned ineptitude with my camera, I performed the multi-limbed manure-fly dance called whitey-swats-a-fly. Anyone seeing a video would have guessed that my scene and the scene featuring the singing women were shot at two separate locations and then super-imposed on one another in the editing room. Their scene was shot in the Library of Congress. My scene was filmed just after I attacked a hive of killer bees with a golf club.

Sometime between the 13th and 14th chorus I heard a camera click and we moved on to the fire-starting demonstration. A warrior twirled a hardwood stick into a piece of softwood and actually got a fire going amid dried leaves. Then, it was my turn. When I appeared to be having trouble, one of the less patient warriors snatched the hardwood stick out of my hand and squatted. He soon found out what my problem was. It was the suntan lotion, 2 millimeters thick, that I had applied to my face, neck and hands post fly-episode.

His luck was no better than mine and I believe it might have cost him a wife or two in status.

They have multiple wives depending on their success at cattle raising. Twenty cattle will get you a young pretty wife; fifteen will get you a fairly nice wife and ten will get you one that looks like Walter Cronkite with pierced ears. I'm serious. I saw him/her.

There is a tragic problem currently among the Masai. It seems some older men have been saving their cattle and buying 12 year old girls. Considering that Africans in general hit adolescence 2 to 3 years later than Americans, it is truly cradle-robbing. This sociological epidemic has even made the Kenyan newspapers.

Besides owning cattle, you must be a warrior to get into the Masai wife-o-rama. To be a warrior you must have killed a lion with a spear. No dead lion, no wife. I'm actually okay with it but let's do the math. There are some 400,000 Masai and only 20,000 lions in their semi-nomadic territory. So somebody is either lying about his hunting exploits ("It was a big one but the elephants ate it after I speared it") or about 380,000 guys are taking the Masai equivalent of a cold shower.

I bought some stuff. I am an archer and I make my own English long bows. I really wanted a Masai bow and some arrows but I was not going to buy the beaded junk set out by the women or sold in gift shops to dazzle tourists. I asked the chief if he still used a bow and arrow. He said he uses them. He usually hunts at close range with arrows dipped in neurotoxin. I asked him to show me his gear. He went into his hut and emerged with a plain wooden bow and well-used leather quiver. It was a tube-like holder with a strap and leather cap. The arrows were about three fifths the length of American arrows and they had beaten metal arrow heads.

He demonstrated shooting and then he let me try. His simple, straight bow was amazingly hard to pull. A strong warrior could send an arrow hundreds of yards.

I was convinced. I told him I wanted to buy his bow, arrows and neat little leather quiver. He said they had some at another place for sale. I told him I wanted his bow and offered him twenty five hundred shillings for it (about $35 US). He removed all but three arrows from the quiver and took the money. He showed me how it was to be tied and told me how to break it in because it was less than three months old and hardly used. I was delighted.

I also bought a war club – a nasty little head knocker that all Masai men carry. In addition, I bought one of their long milk gourds. In this they put a small amount of charcoal and fill it with milk. It is purported to keep for two weeks without spoiling. Yum.

The Masai diet consists of meat, milk and fresh blood. When I told them I was a vegetarian they laughed and made contemptuous comparisons to various dull witted, sissy, prey-animals of the herbivore persuasion.

At this juncture, we were within a reasonable distance of the Land Rover so I pointed out what sort of animals eat dead meat (hyenas and buzzards) as well the fact that babies drink milk and mosquitoes like fresh blood.

There was silence except for the distant sound of the 27th verse of the women's welcoming song.

I just want to point out another mathematical fact to all you carnivores: For every time you have come across a vegetarian and given him a hard time, we have had about a hundred opportunities to spar previously. We're ready for you with or without your Masai head knocker.

One other interesting item of information about the Masai involved some herbal lore. They had plants to stop bleeding, treat infection, cure pain and so forth. When I said I would like something to ward off the flies, the chief walked over, picked a few leaves from a dull looking plant, crushed the leaves and told me to rub this on my skin.

Now, this was before the carrion-eater, baby milk-drinker, mosquito crack so I still trusted his motives. It worked! Either the flies were going along graciously with the placebo effect or it was for real. I like that kind of thing being added to my little store of odd-and-interesting facts.

Even though I could never find that plant again to save my life.

This should have been paradise. I was soon to find it to be a battleground between the forces of good and evil. Pictured here are two homes on the same plot – one for each wife. Both wives must fix him dinner.

Peter's six children dressed up for a picture. The whole family slept in half of the 10 X 10 hut in the background. This was taken after one week of various treatments. We had some smiles going by then.

Traffic jam. This is the broad path outside of where I slept each night and where I brushed my teeth each morning. Most of these people were on their way to and from the water sources. The donkeys were loaded with dried corn for the posho mills where it's ground into gritty flour which is then made into edible hockey pucks.

This is actually worse than it looks. The cattle are confused, the villager is horrified and I am on a zigzag going sideways. We later changed to a 4-ox model.

Skinny arms and big stomachs indicate worms. Even the mother is infected. This was one of several families I treated for many ailments. They have no access to medicine other than tribal witchdoctors.

Western doctors, who had been through the village previously, mistook these symptoms as signs of malnutrition.

The worms weaken the children and elderly making them susceptible to worse infections and death.

Infant mortality for children under 5 is between 40 and 50%.

A Mzungu (me) attempts to protect his thin European teeth while gnawing sugar cane. When I was finished I was covered in syrup. The children wisely sat four or more feet away.

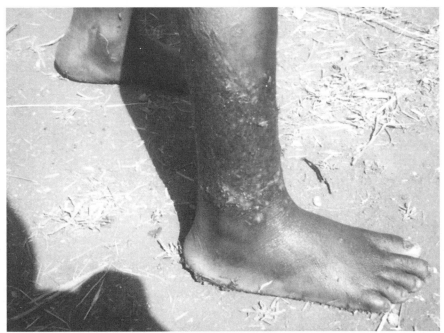

One of the scarier ailments I had to treat. I had never seen it before.

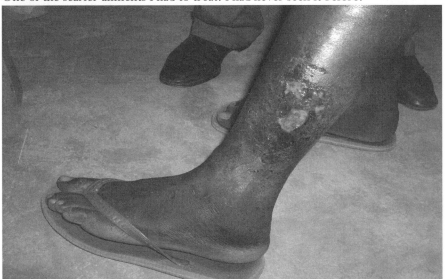

This is a mild case of leg ulceration — very manageable. Some of the ones I treated were four times as large and up to ½" deep. Gramacin powder and no bandages for you Western MD's planning to visit Africa.

While measuring the flow rate of the river for potential hydro-electric output, I was displaced several times by small herds being driven in to drink. Further downstream were children splashing and swimming. I'm thinking this is not well chlorinated.

These guys were everywhere. If you think it's traumatic hitting a deer with your VW, try one of these. Despite the villagers' assertions and my weak defense, these are not found roaming the suburbs of Seattle. One more thought: I know zoologists will tell you their stripes evolved for camouflage, but I think God painted them this way because it looks silly. You need to smile now and then in the agony we call Africa.

Matatu: the most common transportation outside the village. There are 14 people in the cab plus one hanging out the back. This is a small Toyota pick-up with a custom cabin. No air-conditioning. I don't know how the passengers survive.

. The Chief and the Number 2 Man of the Masai village at the northern tip of the Serengeti (Masai Mara). It's as dry as it looks. They invented the original Atkins Diet: meat, milk, blood, nothing else.

A few of the ladies who sang a multi-versed welcome song, barefooted amid the cattle dung. Masai women traditionally pose with their heads tilted up. Their homes are in the background – the Serengeti suburbs, so to speak. They are built in a fenced circle to keep the lions out.

Below shows the relative size of a hut.

I actually think warthogs are cute. But then I own a bulldog named Bullard. Warthogs have better tails.

Bullard, my bulldog waited patiently for me to come home and he didn't do the typical dog guilt thing when I walked in. As you can see, he's pretty happy to have me back.

Chapter Eleven
Dr. Mzungu's First Follow-up Visits

Your medicine is not helping," the angry father barked at me as I approached his hut. His daughter, Lisa was the one dying of pneumonia. "She is sicker than she was. She needs more medicine."

These people have no real sense of the mechanisms by which antibiotics and other medicines effect cures. Even educated Americans don't realize that an antibiotic doesn't kill *all* the germs. It just kills and weakens enough of them that your body is no longer overwhelmed and can finish the job. To the villagers, if a little is good, then a lot is better. If the first pill doesn't work, take two the next time. For this reason, I doled out the medicine one or two days at a time.

"Let me look at Lisa." They brought her out. She *was* worse. I tried to get a response from her. "How are you honey?" I asked. She opened her eyes and looked at me and then she coughed. I watched in horror as her eyes rolled back in her head. Lisa was dying. The father had every right to be demanding.

"Give her some more medicine," he insisted menacingly.

"I'm not going to give her more medicine. Lisa has a very different kind of disease. The bacteria that are making her sick hide in her where the medicine can't get to them. They come out every once in a while. It takes a long time to kill them." I tried as best I could to explain this particular bacterium's odd habit of going inside the cell like a virus to replicate and then coming out of the cell where it seeks out another weak cell to invade. It was at that point that the antibiotics had to be in the blood stream to weaken or kill the bacteria.

"We will have to wait another couple of days. I will come back."

I could tell the mother was feeling better, although she insisted the medicine had not helped. I pushed in the middle of her back, well above the kidneys. "Does this still hurt?" She listened to her husband translate and then she nodded her head yes. I knew she was fibbing. She just wanted more medication. Performing this kind of medicine is worse than being a veterinarian. A vet can't talk to the animals and that's a real disadvantage. But then again, a dog never tries to lie to a vet and give him phony symptoms.

The father approached me as I checked out the girl who had had a painful ear ache for which I had given her the African version of Keflex. She did not lie. It was feeling much better for the first time in several weeks. When I completed the checkup, he grabbed my shoulder and pointed to his three year old, Lisa. As he opened his mouth to make yet another demand, I held up my hand to stop him.

"Look, if you don't like seeing your kids sick, then dig your family a pit latrine. You said you would. They're going into the woods like a bunch of animals and getting worms from each other. I'm not the problem. You are. Now do something about it."

I left. I never felt so right in my life.

At the house of gangrene, I examined Sarah's leg. I couldn't tell what I was looking at. A blackish disease on dark brown skin is hard. I cleaned it thoroughly again but this time I left the gauze and wrap off. "Let's see how this works." I looked up at the little girl as I rubbed the new antibiotic ointment on it. She smiled. Sarah trusted me. That made one of us. I said a silent prayer. It was a very earnest prayer of helplessness.

When I got home I was troubled. I felt useless. I sat on the porch and prayed again. I looked up and a woman was walking her thirteen year old son toward me. "Cha-lees," she called my Luo name. "Can you look at my son? They sent him home from school."

Her son stood before me in the sun as I looked him over. He had small bumps on his face. "How old is he?" I asked. This looked like adolescence to me.

"He is thirteen."

That sounded about right for what looked like acne. But then I thought, "Why would they send him home from school? Surely they have seen acne before." Something wasn't adding up. A veterinarian friend of mine had once told me to make the simplest diagnosis and you would be right ninety per cent of the time. His expression was, "When you hear hoof beats, it's not zebras." It was ironic that I would recall that statement now that I was in Africa where it could be zebras.

"I've got to tell you, Syvietta, I'm not sure. It kind of looks like acne." As the words left my mouth I realized that at age 13 he was still two or more years from African adolescence.

"Is there anything else he's complaining about? Aches, pains, fevers?"

She pointed to his arms. It looked like the same bumps. Now I was thinking allergies. But what bothered me was the question of why he would have bumps on his arms and not on his legs or thorax if it was an allergy? I looked at his gums. They seemed pale. As I glanced down in thought, I noticed that he had a bumpy look between his fingers.

"Well, Cha-lees?" she asked patiently.

"I'm stumped but I'm not completely without a plan." I went inside and came out with two tubes. "We're going to put a strong antibiotic ointment on one cheek and a steroid ointment on the other. We'll see if he responds to either. If not, we go the allergy route."

"Do you think that will cure it?"

"No, I don't, Syvietta. I'm stumped. Let me ask you, did anyone else get sent home?"

Yes, three other boys"

"Same thing?"

"I don't know."

"Same day?"

She asked him the question and he nodded yes.

"That helps. It tells me it's an infectious issue possibly. Tell me about this school."

"It is a very bad high school but it is all we can afford."

"What does it cost?"

"One hundred dollars for three months."

This was not encouraging. How could they afford to even feed the kids for that amount? That was a troubling question so I asked the child what he ate. He wouldn't answer so she intervened.

"He gets corn and bread and potatoes."

"Any fruits or vegetables?"

"Almost none."

"Well then why do you send him there?"

"It is all we can afford. He must get his high school or he will never have a chance." She started to puddle up and a tear rolled down her cheek. The child looked at the ground in shame.

"Syvietta, I'm sorry. I was not aware and I shouldn't question such things. I am going to Kisumu and I will ask someone about this."

She nodded and the two left in silence. This had been a very hard day.

I climbed in the car the next morning as we headed to Kisumu. I thought about everything I was doing with these sick people. The number I was treating now exceeded forty. Who the heck was *I*? Still, I reviewed everything I was doing and while I would have loved to have seen pink tongues and handsprings in the yard, I still believed the treatments were correct. What bothered me was the downside of being wrong. When you make a mistake fixing your car it's a lot different set of consequences. Children don't lose their legs or die when you accidentally replace an alternator instead of the voltage regulator. But kids with pneumonia and gangrene go down fast when you give them the wrong pills for too long. This was serious and I had no earthly assistance. The people wouldn't go to the doctors and the doctors wouldn't touch Kodera.

In Kisumu, my prayers, my many prayers, were answered. I went to a large pharmacist shop in the middle of town. It was very professional. I picked the one guy with a white lab coat and sat at the counter with him. We discussed each of my cases. He was a terrific resource. His other job was working at the Provincial hospital, treating rural cases when they made their way to the big city. He had seen a little of everything.

When I got to the neighbor with the acne-like bumps, the pharmacist knew right away what it was. It was infectious. It would respond slightly to the antibiotic but not enough to effect a cure. The disease was scabies. It is a parasite that enters in through the skin, typically in the space between the fingers and makes its way all through your hands, arms, face and neck and then down through your thorax and so on. He got me a tube of Scabalon. I told him about the malnutrition side of it. He listened patiently as I told him my theory that almost all the diseases in Kodera were due to either worms or malnutrition. Everything was apparently a secondary infection and I was always aiming at the reflection not the image. He liked that expression and wrote it down. He then told me he agreed with me completely.

"I have one more thing for you." He arose and went back to the large stock room. He returned with a small white envelope. I looked inside at the single, brown gelatin capsule that looked like a giant vitamin E soft gel.

"It looks like it's missing its threads."

"What's that?" he asked.

"Nothing. It's a football comment. American football. This thing is huge. What is it?"

"When you send kids to a poor school, they don't eat anything with any vitamin A in it. After a while their liver quits working right. This is a re-activator of sorts. It is 200,000 units of vitamin A."

"Vitamin A or beta carotene?"

"At this point, beta carotene won't do him a whole lot of good, since his liver isn't making the conversion to vitamin A."

I had studied vitamin A precursor conversion and I knew this was serious. "It sounds like he could die."

"Children do die. They never say it's a vitamin A deficiency. They just…die."

I thanked him as I gathered up the medications. He affirmed my treatment of the gangrene and pneumonia patients. He touched my shoulder and said, "These people will die if you give up, Charles."

"At some point, I go home, you know."

"And when you do…"

What an awful burden. Dealing in such truths when real people were involved was like carrying around a refrigerator. You are always aware of the burden. You need a rest now and then.

He told me to have the family boil all their clothes or the scabies would re-establish itself. I later took the family through a complete plan to treat the scabies and then told them they needed to supplement his food with some fresh fruits and vegetables. By the way, the pharmacist was right. The day after the boy had applied the Scabion and had taken the vitamin A, the symptoms disappeared.

In Kenya there are some wonderful people who really know what they are doing. Poorly paid people show up to work every day and save lives. They work in silence and no one ever says thanks. I never followed up with this pharmacist but I will see him again, some day, Lord willing, and shake his hand. I'll find a meaningful way to say thank you.

Chapter Twelve
Bridgette

It was morning in Kenya and we were driving the dirt back roads to Kisii. This was a filthy town and I hated being there. But it was the only town within hours where I could get medicine and some rudimentary supplies.

Driving to Kisii held another element of displeasure for me. It was the only place where the word for white man, Mzungu, was used in a derisive way. Each time I drove to Kisii I got dirty looks and at least 20 "Mzungu's" sent my way. Everybody knew the Kisii were less friendly than the average Kenyan. No one knew this better than I.

As we approached the paved road section, we passed a woman on crutches. She had only one leg. She was dressed in a classy, pleated wool skirt, rayon blouse and a wool blazer. She was about 26 years old and her crutches looked to be in bad shape. We stopped and backed up. She hopped in the car. No words were exchanged.

I leaned over to Christopher, "Do you know her?" He shook his head no. We drove for another couple of minutes in silence.

Finally, I couldn't sit quiet any longer. I decided to start indiscreetly and work back. I asked her if she spoke English. She did. Her name was Bridgette. She seemed pleasant and very intelligent.

"Tell me what life is like in a Kisii village with only one leg. How did you lose your leg, if I may ask?"

"It was bitten by a puff adder when I was out in a corn field."

"A puff adder doesn't have enough venom to cost you a leg."

"Well, it got infected and then I got gangrene. Eventually, they had to cut off my leg."

People, even in America, don't realize that a venomous bite of any kind, including a bee sting or a spider bite, causes significant exposure. The body goes through such an effort to fight off the venom that it opens the way for opportunistic bacteria to enter. They can enter anywhere because your immune system is overtaxed. Often times, wasp bites cause pneumonia. Many doctors are now prescribing antibiotics prophylactically and adding a 5, 4, 3, 2, 1 steroid treatment to speed healing and close the door on evil stuff getting a foothold.

"So what's life like? Is it hard?"

Christopher interjected, "Of course it's hard. What do you think? She only has one leg."

Christopher did not fully understand the subtlety of asking a question that opens a door for someone to emote and say what they may have been storing up for years. Africans ask direct questions. They answer as asked, when speaking African to African. I shrugged him off and looked back at her expectantly. She began slowly.

"It is sometimes very hard. I live with my mother and she does most of the work. Most of the time she can go get the water from the spring. It takes her over an hour for each round trip but she can use the 20 liter (five gallon) bucket. But on days when she is ill, I must go and get the water."

"How do you do that, Bridgette?" I asked, trying to imagine what it would be like to carry a bucket of water on crutches.

"I cannot use the large bucket. I have an eight liter (2 gallon) bucket and I must make several trips. When my mother is sick I spend over 10 hours just getting water. On rainy days, it is horrible. I slip so many times and I lose the water coming up the hills. On those days we just can't get all the water. We don't wash. We only cook and eat."

I tried to make eye contact as she spoke but she just looked out the window. She was so beautiful. In America, she would have had men fighting to be with her for just one evening out. Here, she was a less productive utility and less likely ever to have the support of a man. She was stuck in a mud hut in Kisii.

"So why are you going into Kisii Town?"

"Two reasons. One is, today they will have my new crutches. These are becoming impossible. The end caps are gone and the legs are bending. They will break off soon."

They were, in fact, the cheapest looking metal crutches I had ever seen. "What's the other reason?"

"I can sometimes get part time work at the Coca Cola distributor in Kisii. It really helps make the difference on food. We never have surplus food."

"Were you going to take a matatu today?"

"Yes. That is where I was going."

"How can you stand to ride in those things?"

"It is awful. Many times they just drop us all off at the edge of the city and we all must walk more than three kilometers while they turn around to pick up new passengers. There is nothing we can do."

We dropped her off at the marketplace, near Kisii General Hospital. Christopher pulled out into traffic. I looked back and saw her turn to face us and then come toward us. Then she stopped. For a moment she was poised and calm. The next moment she was stumping after us on cheap metal crutches that skidded and gave way. I told Christopher she was coming after us. He peeked in his rear view mirror but did not slow down. "She's not coming," he said, dismissing my concern. I looked back and indeed she had somehow disappeared. "She went to the hospital," Christopher drove on.

"But I saw her," I thought to myself. "She wanted something." We continued driving and went on about our business in Kisii.

Later as we were pulling into a filling station to get some petrol for tomorrow's long drive, I saw Bridgette at the door of a matatu, her old crutches in her hand. I tried to get out of my car but another matatu pulled up so close to my car, I couldn't open my door. I rolled down my window and called her name. She saw me and waved with a gracious smile."

I yelled, "Where are your new crutches?"

"Not here yet," she yelled back, as a matatu driver pushed her hard in the small of her back. Bridgette bowed backwards and then the driver shoved her into the van. I yelled at the matatu driver parked next to me to get away from my door so I could get out. He ignored me, so I leaned out of my window and slapped his windshield hard. That woke him up. He shifted gears and backed up slowly.

I was frantic to get to her and get her out of that matatu. I had thought about her all morning. I could get her help: A prosthetic for her leg, some money. We could certainly give her a ride and talk about a plan on the way back to her home. I could have picked up the tab on the crutches.

The matatu she was in pulled away before I could get out and get to her. I saw her get smooshed to one side of the packed matatu. This classy woman was forced to live a horrible existence and I was doing nothing. The memory of her being jammed to one side of the matatu and reaching back for her crutches while looking back at me still troubles me terribly. I didn't do anything.

Why didn't I think to get her mailing information on the ride in? Was I not aware of my ability to offer financial assistance or was I hanging on to my money out of instinct and learning to inure myself to the human devastation all around me? What was I thinking when someone in such clear need sat in our car for almost a half hour? I hated myself.

On the way home I thought about Sarah, the brave little girl I was treating for gangrene. God had just given me a preview of what would happen if I missed the mark. I was playing with fire and I had no one to pass it off to. I couldn't even chicken out. I was truly stuck in the middle of this ordeal with myself as my only company. This was Genesis 41:16 time. Still, as I type these words and I think of Bridgette fighting for her existence on one leg, I'm haunted. I wake up nights reaching for that matatu. There are moments when I hate myself.

My parting memory of that day was hearing a song coming from a neighboring car, in the middle of Kisii. It was the last verse of Bob Dylan's "My Back Pages" – a song whose words never made a whole lot of sense to me but in a strange way they fit that day:

Yes, my guard stood hard when abstract threats

Too noble to neglect

Deceived me into thinking

I had something to protect

Good and bad, I define these terms

Quite clear, no doubt, somehow.

Ah, but I was so much older then,

I'm younger than that now.

The marketplace at Kisii where we dropped Bridgette off to make her way to the hospital.

Chapter Thirteen
More Road Stories

Let me tell you about the Roho. As you drive the rural routes of western Kenya, you may occasionally come across a troop of people, dressed mostly in white, wearing chef-like caps with red, Christian crosses on them. They often jog great distances to nowhere in particular, singing very rhythmic, very African sounding songs. Often these songs are in a split chorus and responsive between a leader and the troop.

Despite their outward appearance with the cross and all, they have their own religion. They do not hold Jesus Christ as deity. They instead appear to be an entirely separate religion that pulls bits here and there from various sources, one of which is the Bible.

It is not a form of syncretism. Sikhism in India is a syncretic religion. It was formed to solve two problems: the militancy of the Muslims and the class system of the Hindus which put people in categories with Brahmans on top and untouchables on the bottom.

Roho appears to solve no such problem, socially or politically. While in Kenya I came across two different Roho sects: Roho Israel and Roho Msanda. Roho means spirit both in Swahili and the local Luo dialect. Roho Israel is short for Roho Israel Nineveh, perhaps for the town in Tyre that repented upon hearing the reluctant prophet Jonah's teachings and warnings.

Roho Msanda is another sect whose custom it is, as it is with Roho Israel, to pray directly to God and not in the name of Christ. They have some interesting religious beliefs but the most readily apparent (and annoying) aspect of Roho Msanda is their prohibition against shaking hands. This would be tough enough in Western society but it is unthinkable in amicable, handshaking Luo Land. When you reach to shake hands, a Roho Msanda will step back, smile and clap his hands lightly to signal he will not be shaking your hand.

The first time this happened to me I turned to the interpreter and asked if the Roho had a contagious disease and if was he getting treatment. The interpreter laughed and explained the Roho don't shake hands as part of their religion.

Let's put this in perspective. When you walk down a road in Luo land and you see 22 people you might know only a little, you will shake hands 22, 44 or 66 times depending on how long you talk and if you get interrupted in saying good bye. If someone comes up to your car, he will shake hands with the driver and each of the passengers, coming and going, whether he knows them or not. As I have mentioned, when a husband comes home at night or after being away on a trip, the first thing he will do is shake hands with his wife and then each of his children.

Upon finding out the extent of this custom, I soon protected myself from what I knew to be overall bad hygiene. Since I am a man, I could always expect to ride in the front of the car while someone else drives. In the side pocket I stashed a pump bottle of Purell waterless hand cleaner, family size. I used it at least five times every drive. I was polite enough to wait until I was out of sight and then I performed my ablutions d' mzungeaux.

I considered converting to Rohoism every time I walked down a road without my Purell pump bottle. But I remembered that being clean on the outside while being ungodly on the inside got the Pharisees in a heap of trouble. I like the Roho's singing and I admire their pluck in not shaking hands in Luo land. However, just like all sects based on some guy with a couple of clever ideas but no heritage linked to God, it doesn't make a lot of sense. Perhaps this is why it remains a small, obscure sect in East Africa.

Free Churches

As we drove north, just past Rongo, I saw one of the largest, nicest churches I had seen in Kenya. It was directly across the highway from a compound of nicer houses in an estate setting. The house in the very center of the estate compound was the home of the former Chief of District Administrators under the corrupt Moi regime. This man had once held great power. Since each administrator in every district reported to him, they owed their lifestyle and existence to him. It is said that when he called on the telephone, the district administrator receiving the call would stand and salute over the telephone. This was done just in case an onlooker was to report that he had taken the Chief's call too casually. Shades of Stalin. And there is some more in common with the Stalin era.

It seems the Chief Administrator was very close to Moi. At the height of the Moi era in the early 90's, Moi requested to meet with George Bush Sr. Bush knew of the fetid state of affairs in Kenya and refused to meet with him. However, he did offer to hold council with a Kenyan of honorable repute named Robert Ouko. When Ouko met with Bush, details of Kenya's extensive corruption were revealed. Bush made an off hand comment that Kenya would be better off if Ouko were president.

When Ouko got off the plane in Nairobi, there were several Moi associates to greet him. One asked Ouko, "How are you, Mr. President?" Robert Ouko knew he was in trouble. Some time later a group of men came to Ouko's house and asked him to come to a meeting.

An hour's drive away, they pulled over and murdered Ouko and then burned his body. According to local gossip, the Chief Administrator was the lead conspirator. Under President Kibaki, Moi's replacement, the original inquest has been reactivated. The original inquest had fallen apart due to too much press coverage.

In the meantime, the Chief Administrator had taken on his third wife, which he could well afford under Moi. His only error in bride selection was in choosing women from three separate Christian denominations. To resolve this he used government money to build each wife a new church of rather glorious architecture.

These churches are built with money stolen from the people of Kenya. I'm wondering if this is the moral foundation of sand which Christ warned people not to build upon. In truth, I'm not wondering at all. Compromises with pagan customs and an immoral government are common in Kenya just as they are in the Western world. They just lack the well developed wisdom that modern American churches often perfume themselves with.

There will be a day of reckoning for all such compromised churches. Their stories may be interesting and their architecture might be striking but I would like to be standing at least a sugar cane field away when God has had his fill.

The Roho

Chapter Fourteen
The Teeth of the Luo

It wasn't long after arriving in Kodera and wandering along the more remote trails that I noticed a strange matter of dentition. It appeared only among some of the villagers. They were missing their lower six teeth – the four little incisors and the two neighboring eye teeth (incorrectly called canines by carnivores who have never looked in a dog's mouth). Having used my lower teeth in my attempts to join Kenyan children in stripping the outer covering off of sugar cane, I could well imagine how this might happen. Still, I was seeing it too often and only in the older villagers. I couldn't blame it on sugar cane.

One day as I was out for a morning walkabout, I saw two men plowing a field. One of them was in his early 60's. I walked up to them and told them I had always wanted to try my hand at plowing behind a couple of oxen. Each had a little smile on his face as they agreed to my proposition. They gave me a few instruction in Luo (English would not have made a difference). The way it works is to have one man crack the whip and motivate the two oxen while the other works the plow, a wooden v-shaped apparatus with a single metal blade.

By the time I was ready to be Great White Farmer, a fair crowd had gathered and was watching in silence. I nodded and the oxen took off. They walked straight to begin with but soon my zigzagging and general destruction of the farmer's morning work pulled them sideways. The onlookers along with both the farmer and driver were rolling on the ground laughing. I tried twice more but the cattle began to get disgusted and they wouldn't go anymore.

The crowd huddled to confer. After they recovered and wiped the tears from their eyes, they began to analyze the problem. The conclusion: when a plowman was as unskilled as I, he must dig the plow in deeper if there is any hope of not skipping over the furrows the way I was. This would require four oxen. Soon, I was part of a large party wandering through the fields of Kodera to find a four ox team. We found one. The effect was the same except the zigs and zags were more pronounced and they happened a lot faster. Oh, one other difference with the four-ox episode: the laughter was more pronounced because we had picked up another dozen or so onlookers.

I offered the plow back to the farmer. He did not take it but instead wiped his brow and took a break from laughing. Soon I found myself surrounded by a large group of people who just wanted to chat. As we stood and talked and shared lots of laughs, I spotted again the shiny hard lower gums of the elderly Luo men and women. I had to ask. Silence immediately settled in. This lasted for a bit as a few feet shuffled. It seems no one talks about this, a fact I confirmed later when I spoke to villagers in their 20s who really did not know the details.

To break the silence I told one I the old plowman if he didn't tell me the history, I'd go back and plow his field again. This brought a laugh and broke the ice. I got the whole story:

In days long ago, all children at the edge of adolescence were required to go through two public initiation rites: circumcision and teeth extraction. Under both procedures, the slightest flinch or sound would bring instant shame and would haunt you the rest of your life. Even a twitch or a wince under the blade of the circumciser would be the end of your manhood, not the beginning. (Female circumcision is another topic altogether with its own horror stories, still being played out throughout Africa).

I wanted the details. I could imagine how the circumcision worked but dentistry is a complex matter. In a village with no door knobs and strings, not to mention dental tools, I was struggling to figure out how tooth extraction worked.

There is a flat knife with a dull blade in the shape of a dagger that they use for the procedure. First, the knife point is inserted sideways between the teeth and twisted. This loosens the incisors with their shallow roots. The eye teeth require twisting from both sides and generally more work. Next, the point is inserted in the gum space, below and next to the tooth. The first incisor is tough they all agreed but nothing compared to the eye teeth. Once they get the point deep enough it is bent back and forth until the tooth, the perfectly good tooth, snaps loose while the mouth fills with blood.

I would have been required to be strapped to a heavy chair and all my limbs duct-taped to the legs and arm rests. They did not have chairs or duct tape so I asked how they were positioned for this ritual. What did they do while the extraction-meister was plucking teeth? As soon as my question was interpreted, three men and one woman simultaneously held one arm straight down to their side and the other arm reached behind their backs and grasped the straight arm tightly. They took one step to the side and held their head up and opened their mouths. There was a ritual position! And that was how they stood some 40 years ago, in a clearing, in front of the whole village.

I asked if this practice had its roots in anything that made sense. They insisted it did. This I had to hear.

Hundreds of years ago, a common way to die was lockjaw. Tetanus remains a killer in rural Africa, even today. Unfortunately, tetanus at first just makes you feel horribly weak and chilled like a very bad flu. I know, I've had it but I got to the hospital in time. The only way you could really know for sure someone had tetanus, rather than a flu or a bout of malaria, is when lockjaw sets in during the last phase.

The Luo had a root extract they would feed someone with tetanus, provided they could diagnose it in time. Once the jaws clamp it is almost impossible to get them open. I worked with a Philippine physician for a year at the UW Hospital who told me rural medicine stories that were simply medieval. One was the story of all the implements they had tried using to open the jaws of a man with lockjaw. He had contracted the disease by poking his finger on a fish spine. They failed and he died. The ancient Luo had had similar failures.

However, if the teeth are missing and a gap is available, they can shove in the plant extract mixed with porridge and force the victim to swallow. This resulted in a much higher survival rate. It was decided that all Luo should have their teeth extracted. It was ritualized and that was the story. Fortunately, as missionaries brought medicine, the tetanus shot was introduced. Shots and boosters last about ten years.

No one knows exactly when this practice stopped. One other tribe in central Kenya has a similar practice but only removes two teeth. Both tribes appear to have let this mandatory ritual slip into desuetude some time in the mid to late 60's. There was no edict of cessation. I judged by the ages of the people who had the gap to make my determination. However, it is evidently still being practiced among some Luo tribes in the Sudan. This is thought to be the case because one of the villagers came across a Sudanese Luo in his early twenties in Nairobi. When the man smiled he revealed six missing lower teeth.

It is in vogue right now to show a degree of disdain for Western medicine. I agree that the pendulum has swung too far to pills and surgery when nutrition and some old world techniques may be better. This is especially true for chronic problems such as arthritis, eczema, and others. However, when it comes to infectious diseases, vaccines and trauma, nothing beats American medicine. No one in Kenya complains about getting a DPT shot. Consider the alternative procedure I just described.

| |||||||||||||||||

While on the subject of teeth, I want to mention the subject of sugar cane. It's all about teeth. One Saturday, I asked Isaiah, the eleven-year old son in the home where I stayed, if he wanted to go get some sugar cane. He was excited. It's a treat even though they can get it all year round.

Isaiah is an extremely bright and precocious child. If he were here in America he could be class valedictorian, provided he did not get caught up in the new youth culture which celebrates failure and disassociates itself from anything good and meaningful. Isaiah was imminently trainable on almost anything that I attempted to tutor him on from math to geography to medicine. On a number of my house visits, he acted as my translator. I had full trust in him.

When it came time to go to the market and select some sugar cane, I wanted him to go with me. It all looked like bamboo to me. We walked less than a mile before coming to the market. The three women recognized me for being "not one of them" and immediately offered an eight foot stalk of sugar cane from the pile. Isaiah knew they were offering worst first. With the edge of his sandals he sorted through the pile and repeatedly refused suggestions by the women. Finally, he picked two stalks from two different piles. He was very careful because sugar cane is like fine wine to them, there is a big difference in stalks and they can tell. You are also criticized for bringing home bad cane.

When they told me the price, one said 12 shillings and the other said 20. Isaiah told me it was only 12. I turned to the one asking 20 and asked, "Is it normally only 12?" She became rattled when she saw me hand the honest woman 50 shillings, refusing change. Now the over-charger was really perplexed and I was a bit troubled as well because I always paid extra but I hated rewarding dishonesty. "I need your best answer." She admitted she had overcharged. I gave her 50 and then went to the third lady and asked her to pick out the best one and to not give me a Mzungu stalk. She smiled and reached to the bottom. Isaiah nodded and I handed her 50 shillings.

I then handed each of them 200 shillings and told them that some day someone would come along who could not afford sugar cane. If they were to give someone free sugar cane who could not afford it, they could keep the money. I asked if that was fair. It was one of those experiments for which I would never see the results but for which there was no way to lose. Besides, it cost less than ten dollars.

Back at home, Isaiah washed the stalks and then grabbed a machete. I am amazed at the dexterous handling of a machete by even tiny African children. He offered me the thick base end. I found out later it is the best end. Soon we were mysteriously surrounded by a half dozen kids I had never seen before. They waited patiently while Isaiah cut them each a two foot section. Then we all sat in a semi-circle and ate sugar cane. It was sweet and juicy and almost floral tasting. Everyone, including me laughed and smiled a lot. This was Garden of Eden-level innocence and mirth.

The husk surrounding the juicy fibers is exactly like bamboo. My thin European teeth were scarcely a match and I had to use a knife to split it up. I expected to yank off a long strip and see my teeth go flying. They on the other hand could shred a two-by- four piece of lumber with their thick white teeth. I later asked a group of children and their parents if they had ever been to a dentist. Most had not. The ones that did go had no cavities. Only the ethnic Mayans of Central America are truly impervious to dental cavities. These people were not impervious but they were a close second.

Soon the children had each gone through two full pieces of sugar cane. I was still working on my first piece. They left perfectly clean. I looked down and saw juice dripping off my wrist and elbow and saturating my clothes. There was more to this sugar cane thing than they were telling me.

Chapter Fifteen
The Final Wife and a Long Weekend

The car pulled out slowly in the pre-dawn darkness. Christopher was on a mission of mercy. He had been asked to pick up a woman with AIDS who was rounding the final turn. The night before, frantic relatives had come to the house and asked if Christopher would please drive the woman to Kisii hospital. It was 11:30 and Christopher knew what the inside of the Kisii hospital looked like. He also knew how unfriendly the reception would be if he could even get them to open the doors. So he refused to go.

However, the next morning he was up before 5 AM. I was already awake. Before 5:30 the journey had begun. The woman with AIDS was in her parent's house -- "and that is no place for a woman to die," people said, repeatedly. A woman who has been married must die in her marital home. The relatives had now abandoned the idea of going to Kisii hospital. Their visit late last night was just a panicked response to seeing her suffering hit a period of late-stage paroxysm.

She was the third of four wives. The husband and the other three wives had already died of AIDS. That's how it works. If the husband gets AIDS or brings in a new wife with HIV, they all die. In this case, the husband wasn't satisfied with four wives, he went out and found other women to have affairs with and brought the disease back home. AIDS is now beginning to affect statistics. The percent of homes with multiple marriages is plummeting, though the custom remains as strong as ever.

She was transferred from a bamboo cot in one mud hut to another dark mud hut a couple of miles away. Her last stop. She never got to see the cycle that all little girls hope to move through in their lives. She never got to have babies and raise children. She never got to gather with the other elderly women the evening after a good rain and talk about the fortunate days ahead. She had been married less than two years and she was only sixteen years old.

Now, on the drive to her vacant marital home, she spoke with some effort. She asked about the children she expected to see there, sons and daughters of the older wives. These children, now orphans, had long since been passed off separately to various homes of near and not-so-near relatives. She would enter a deserted hut. I was surprised she could talk at all. She was formerly five foot four and 130 pounds. Now she weighed no more than 40 pounds. She was frightening to look upon.

So what were her penultimate words? She wanted her red dress. She feared she had left it behind at her parents' house. She just wanted to look nice and the sack-like garment she was wearing didn't look very good. A woman is a woman right to the end.

It is estimated there will soon be 40 million AIDS orphans in Africa. In the Nyanza Province, where I was working, the villages have an HIV infection rate that goes from a low of 30% to a high in excess of 70%. Each will die, one at a time, mostly in dark, squalid little mud huts. They are conscious and aware to the end; clinging to memories, dreams of what might have been, and the sleeve of a favorite red dress.

The ululations began the following morning. She had died in the night. At 7:30 AM I heard the strange cry from her mother wandering past my dwelling. She made her way up the red clay road to announce to her neighbors, via wailing, that her only daughter had died. A brief period of sympathetic wailing was triggered. It lasted only five minutes that I could hear.

Twenty minutes later, I was in the car on my way to a meeting with the village leadership. As we rounded the corner, the woman I recognized as the mother of the deceased startled me. She turned and extended her arm toward my open window and stopped with her hand out, crying in a subdued wail. Her posture and the way she held her hand said, "Can't you help?" but her face said, "I'm inconsolable." She turned and walked on, to my relief, as the others in the car offered supporting comments in Luo.

One of them explained, "She will cry like that until evening. Tomorrow they will bury her daughter."

This was not the first time I turned and wept silently while looking out the window at what should have been paradise. As we drove I recalled the words of a song. I rarely got a chance to hear music while I was in Kenya. American country western music was even less likely to reach my ears. Though I know only a few country singers and their songs, one stuck in my mind. It was a plaintive tour of a married woman's struggle to stay competitive for her own husband's attention, as time progressed. It was sung by Lorrie Morgan. The final stanza played through my head:

> *I'm looking for something in red*
> *Like the one that I wore when I first turned his head*
> *Strapless and sequined and cut down to there*
> *Just a size larger than I wore last year*
> *A guaranteed number to knock a man dead*
> *I'm looking for something*
> *I've got to have something*
> *I'm looking for something*
> *In red.*

They lowered her into a deep hole in a poorly built casket. She returned to the dirt from which we all were originally wrought. When I looked at the mother, all I could think was, "How could she let her only daughter marry a man who already possessed the daughters of two other women? And she was only sixteen."

I wondered if such thoughts ever entered her mind.

The night before the funeral, I heard drumming coming from the direction of the parents' home. I wanted to add to my "Sounds of Africa" collection so I gathered up my voice-activated tape recorder and started up the road. I could get near the general location of the sound but I could not see where it was coming from exactly. As I crossed out onto the main road, a woman came hurrying toward me from across the path. She greeted me with a hearty handshake. Her

English was OK so I asked her what the drumming was and where it was coming from. She explained that it was the girl's family – the girl who had just died.

"Her funeral is tomorrow," she explained.

"That's very sad." I offered solemnly.

"You take my picture?"

I was a little surprised by this sudden request. It seemed a little out of place. I responded, "Uh, yes. I suppose. I will have to go get my camera." I started off on the quarter mile walk back to my place but she reached over and grabbed me by the wrist and led me in the opposite direction from my home.

"Come. I take you to drumming." She led me through a plowed field onto a path that went around a hut. I came into a clearing behind the hut. It looked like a scene from an old Jungle Jim movie. It was full of people. There were stone fire pits, a pen made of rustic logs surrounding a pair of oxen. To the side, an old man sat before a round cast-iron pot suspended over a wood fire. I entered the clearing and all activity froze.

The father of the deceased walked over and greeted me vigorously and with a smile that bordered on joy. He clasped both my hands and said something in Luo that sounded like a greeting. I returned a quiet, "Mber, ber" – Luo for "Fine, fine" or something very close. The lady who had escorted me told me the father had said a long and formal "Welcome." I turned and said thank you. I then turned back to the woman and asked her to explain at length how sorry I was to hear about his daughter and that I had seen her only recently. She interpreted and he nodded gratefully.

I called the drummer over and asked him to tell me about the drumming. He explained that he was to drum all night and then again very early in the morning. They would bury the AIDS woman tomorrow. He began drumming again. I continued to hold the recorder out of sight as a matter of discretion and politeness. I recorded his drumming.

I felt it best to leave so I thanked them all and indicated to the woman who brought me there that I should go. There is a point at which curiosity crosses the line and I wanted to stay well this side of it.

My escort led the way out of the clearing and as soon as we turned the corner and entered the field, she said, "Take my picture."

I told her I would need to get my camera. She stood at attention and put her arms to her side, head up, posing for all it was worth. I then realized that she had mistaken my metal, hand-held recorder for a camera. I laughed and pointed at it. "Do you think this is a camera?" I asked. She acknowledged as such.

I told her it was a tape recorder. She nodded and started to pose again. I then explained. "This is not a camera." I struggled for a moment and then said, using lots of B movie, African hand gestures, "The camera catches what you see," nod, nod, "This recorder catches what you hear."

She tilted her head back and acknowledged what I had just said with a long "Ohhh."

I felt satisfied right up to the point where she started to pose again. This time I demonstrated. I rewound as I pointed back at the clearing. I hit the play button. The drumming sound was released from the box and she howled with laughter. She then grabbed me by the hand and dragged me back into the clearing full of people. She announced something and the people instantly crowded around me. She gave a brief explanation and they all leaned and turned one ear toward me. There was total silence.

I noticed no one was breathing so I hit the play button. One and a half seconds later, the air was filled with the loudest, most delighted laughter. It looked something like a laugh bomb had just been detonated as a wave of joy pushed the crowd out of the center around me.

Once again, I saluted the old man seated by his cast-iron pot and I strode home alone. There was much to talk about back at the clearing so my former escort remained behind. She was the woman of the hour as the dusky twilight settled over Kodera.

The weekend turned eerie. In a space of less than thirty six hours, eight more people died. None of them was over 40 years old. It felt like Satan was firing silent mortars and making direct hits. The people who died were all within 75 yards of my dwelling. I wanted to plug my ears and duck some place as the pronouncements came in hushed obituaries. Two men died of AIDS; one woman died of something she got when she failed to boil her water; one died of a cancer she had been fighting for almost a year. A baby died at the end of its first bout with malaria, pneumonia took down a perfectly healthy 30 year old man, and no one knows why the others died.

The wailing sessions were concatenated since so many mourners were either related or were close friends. One wailing party continued briefly as a new group got started. The sound came in sine waves, rekindling memories of the air raid drills that used to frighten us when we were children. The ululations began and the drumming followed. It was a very grim weekend.

A number of the men gathered outside and made decisions on who would go to which funeral. Not all could be attended by everyone. It was hot and the bodies needed to be buried quickly. In the towns with electricity, a number of the mortuaries advertised, on hand- written signs, that they have "the best cold room in town." Other mortuaries are *room temperature.*

I sat on a bench in the shade and watched as people came in and out of the yard. Soon I had visitors.

This was getting toward the end of my stay and I had made many friends who now wanted to talk and say something personal before I departed for America. Others knew about me for the medical help I could offer. Still others felt they could come by and tell me about some spiritual or other personal issue and I would listen sincerely and offer a different perspective. I also hold a confidence so I hesitate to share anything here that might threaten that confidence. I had held a similar confidant/counselor position in the workplace back home. Even my political adversaries knew they could talk to me and it would stay in the room. It was often put in this manner, "Ok, Charles, you and I will never agree on a bunch of stuff and in a way I kind of hate your guts but I need to chat with you about a problem. I've been drinking a lot lately and it's really starting to worry me but I can't seem to get on top of it...." I dealt with addictions, adultery, spousal spats, weight loss and financial failure almost on a weekly basis. It turns out, Africans have the very same problems and I got to hear them on my wanderings or during their wanderings – from both men and women.

My first visitor was an elegant woman, with delicate, Somali-like facial features. She had heard about me and wanted to see me. She was out collecting water after attending a couple of funerals, so she went a little out of her way to come and see me. She told me that she wanted to see my blue eyes and yellow hair and she wanted me to write with my left hand and right hand because she had heard that I could do that. I never demonstrated the writing because she excitedly asked me if I wanted to hear a story after we had spoken for only a few minutes. First she had some questions.

"What is the weather like where you come from?"

"Seattle? It's kind of bad. It rains a lot." I forgot we were in the middle of a drought that was delaying planting. People were going to die due to lack of rain. She perked up.

"What kind of crops do you grow? I mean your wife."

"Neither one of us grow any crops."

She was downcast at our inability to take advantage of so much rainfall. I didn't think a lecture on Safeway stores would work well. I had at least learned *something* in these many weeks in Kenya. We spent a moment in contemplation but she was unable to come up with a remedy for our agricultural predicament. Then she looked up at me and said, "I will tell you a story." So she told me the story of Oyango and Omol.

Oyango was a very old man who lived by the river. He was very old. One day he decided to visit his brother.

Omol lived several kilometers up the hill. He walked and he walked. His walking stick was old and bent.

Finally, he came to his brother Omol's house and went in. He told his brother he was visiting to see how he was doing. This made Omol very happy. So they talked. They talked and they talked. Then it began to rain. So after the rain stopped, Oyango got up and left to go back to his home by the river.

He walked until it was just getting dark as he came near his home by the river. When he got next to the river he heard many voices say, "Who are you? Who are you?" This scared Oyango very much so he asked, "Who are you!? And why do you ask an old man who has always lived here 'Who are you?'"

Oyango thought maybe these people were bad men who might be there to kill him. Again, the many voices asked Oyango, "Who are you? Who are you?"

So Oyango yelled, "Help, help! There are people here who wish to harm me!" So the people ran to help Oyango. Some brought spotlights (flashlights to us Westerners) some brought clubs and some brought the machete. They say, "Where is the bad people who want to kill Oyango?"

They look everywhere but they cannot find. Then they come to the river and they see the frogs make the noise with their throats.

When the people saw this they laugh. When Oyango see this he laugh very hard. He even fall down with the walking stick and he laugh very hard.

The woman who told me this could hardly finish the story, she was laughing so hard. "It is an old story but I still laugh very hard," she told me, clutching her sides and doubling over between pneumatic paroxysms.

I missed something.

My only explanation to anyone reading this is that "who are you?" in Luo must sound something like "rivet." But I'm not going to check right away or it will ruin it for me.

She left still laughing. She had an hour's walk ahead of her and I was glad to see her in such a fine mood.

As she left, three men approached for my next meeting. We all greeted in Swahili. One of them went inside and found a two-week old newspaper. The other two remained and we talked. The Luo are exceptional conversationalists.

Word had gotten around that I was leaving soon. A number of these people and I had developed an attachment to one another. I still felt I was about to go on leave while the bullets were still flying. When nine people die in two days in such a small cluster of homes, you know there's a war on. I get R & R. They've got a lifetime enlistment to serve on the front lines.

One of them made a statement after we had been talking for a while that was unrelated to any of our prior topics.

"You know, Cha–lees, there is a very big difference between Americans and all the others who come to Kenya."

"How so?"

"The Germans and the Dutch are very stiff. You can never be their friend. They don't care how you feel and they are not close to you. The Japanese don't even look around or look at the sky. They are in the country to do a project and then they leave. The British think we are not people. They judge us."

"So what do Americans do that's different?"

"Americans talk to you. They care. They ask questions. They make friends with you. They help every way they can. When Dr. Ralph (Aye) was here, he spoke to us just before they left to go back to Nairobi. He said he felt like there was so much work to do and that he was feeling terrible about leaving us. He began to cry and his wife put her arm around his shoulders. We told him we will be okay. Please come back."

He then told me some of the families I had treated were very healthy now and they were not sick for the first time in so very long. He reminded me that some of them could have died without my help, "So please come back and help others."

As we spoke I saw a man walking toward us from a distance. It was a man with horrible leg ulcers, one of several I was treating for this ailment. I was so thankful he had showed up since I didn't know where he lived and I had a new treatment for him.

"I've got some new medicine," I said as I directed him to sit down on a bench near the other men. I went in and got some hydrogen peroxide and gramacin powder. I gloved myself and cleaned the huge ulcers. Then I shook the gramacin powder into the open lakes on his leg. Like a couple of the other leg ulcer patients, he had had these open, raw sores for a number of years now. He looked at me after taking a deep breath on top of some serious reflecting he had been doing.

"I have been told by the missionaries that these are not going to go away. They think it is diabetes."

"What missionaries?" I asked, with a bit of doubt evident.

"I think they are from Finland."

"So you think it's diabetes? What did you have for lunch?"

"Ugali (cornmeal porridge), kale and a cup of chai (tea with milk and sugar).

"How do you feel?"

"Fine."

"Did you have to go to the bathroom a lot?"

"No."

"You don't have diabetes. You look like you have phlebitis. Do you know what phlebitis is?"

"No."

"Bad veins. You have very bad veins. You need an operation. If you don't get some of these stripped out and you keep getting ulcers, you'll get a bad infection some day and then you might die. You've got to realize something, I'm sick of watching people die around here."

I then told him how to take care of his wounds himself. He had to leave them unbandaged and stop going in areas where he might tear them open. "Look, I'm going to be leaving soon. So you have to do the right things to let these heal. But then you have to get them fixed."

He left with the medicine in hand. But something told me he was never going to go to a hospital and take the steps he needed to confirm my diagnosis and get this fixed. He was going to walk around for a few months, maybe years and then be a statistic in a weekend like the one we were all going through now.

As he left the yard, he crossed paths with another man, Michael, heading my way. Michael had left a funeral early because he had remembered his promise to my hosts to bring a chicken to be killed in my honor. I was crestfallen. I had dodged and hemmed and hawed so well these last many weeks. I thought my Chief Joseph strategy had paid off. There would be no sacrifice. I eyed the chicken he was sporting, held by its legs, carried as casually as an umbrella on a cloudy day.

"Michael, that's very nice but does it mean anything when I say, "Mimi sili nyama?" This translates "I don't eat meat."

"But you will eat just a little? It is the custom for a guest."

"I would actually feel a lot better watching the chicken scratch the ground and eat lawn grubs. How do you go about killing him?"

"With a knife, you slice off the head."

"You can't whack it off with a hatchet like they do in cartoons?"

"Hatchet? Cartoons?"

"How about a machete?" I proffered.

"No machete. No need. Just slice with a knife." He demonstrated using a sawing motion.

He took the chicken back to the kitchen and left it on the floor with its feet tied. It looked at me with one beady little chicken eye when I walked past. I felt awful. They looked so happy when they were running around the yard.

About two hours before dinner the next night, I was working on a three foot length of sugar cane and mentally rehearsing my speech. I liked to stand in front of the fire pit and eject spent fiber. About the time I had roughed out a brilliant defense, full of diplomacy, to the scheduled execution of the chicken, I glanced up and saw almost one square meter of fluffy feathers on the edge of the pit. I was too late.

In the last few days, nine people had died and here I was worried about a chicken. Despite what animal rights activists say, animals and humans are a spiritual universe apart from one another. I guess the thing that was bothering me was that it was one more death that I could have in some way worked harder to prevent.

This was a long weekend. I think God gives us all a reservoir we put on our back like a knapsack. Into it we toss a small number of our problems with the intent that we will get back to them later. Some people don't come back to resolve these stored problems. They just keep tossing in new problems. Eventually, there's an overflow that seeps out. We call it depression. If it fills up too fast, it's something beyond depression. I was dangerously close to the "Full" mark.

Chapter Sixteen
More Follow-up Visits

Another visit to the families I was treating was due. I started on my knees in prayer. It was not my skill that was going to set this upright. God had to intervene. I confessed my inadequacy, a task that was getting easier by the day. I was peering out from the God-sized hole I had dug and it was getting harder to see the edge. An "Amen" and a deep breath later and I was off my knees and on the red clay road.

I decided to go to the toughest call first. I approached the hut of Lisa, the pneumonia victim and looked around the yard for children or parents. One would lead to the other eventually. I peered inside, "Hodi, hodi," I called out in Swahili protocol. "Karibu," I heard back. I was surprised. The mother was only skilled in Luo. Swahili was not a language of value for an inveterate village dweller. Her husband knew English and despite his animosity toward me stemming from Lisa's imminent demise, he was helpful in describing symptoms for me.

To my surprise, he was sitting next to his daughter in the dark interior of the hut. He turned to me and in a menacing hiss, said, "She is dying. She needs more medicine."

"I brought more medicine, but it is the same thing as before. She needs to keep taking the very same pills and the very same number of pills."

"She will die. You are letting my daughter die. She needs better pills. Not the same."

"Has there been any change?"

"She is much worse."

"Let's have a look."

We carried the weak, rag doll of a human out to where I could look at her. I pulled open her eyes and listened to her lungs. I took her pulse and then sat on the dirt step that was the entrance to their dusty little home. "I think she is stable. She needs to keep taking the pills." I reached out and handed him the packet of pills I was doling out a couple of days at a time.

"You didn't even take her temperature. Take her temperature. You will see she is very ill. She will need more than that." He eyed my packet of pills with disdain. He rose to his full height of well over six feet. He moved closer and ignored my outstretched hand with the pills.

"Lisa needs these and you need to be patient. I told you this is a different type of illness. It will take a while to get her better." I returned calmly. He did not respond at first. He looked about. We were alone.

"Take her temperature," he said in a flat, measured tone. This was an order.

"I'm not going to do that."

"And why not!?"

"Because it is 95 degrees out. If I take her temperature it will only confirm that it is very hot here in Africa. I already know that. But you will see the temperature and then you'll go berserk trying to get me to give her something else. I'm going to save us both a lot of heartache."

I stood to leave.

"She had better not die," he threatened.

We stood staring at one another for almost twenty seconds. Neither of us blinked. I couldn't fault this man. All he knew was that I was giving his daughter pills and she was still very sick. In a village of 40+% infant mortality, both he and I knew where this might be headed.

"How you doing with that pit latrine?" I asked.

He did not answer.

"I thought so," I said as I walked off.

"She better not die," he repeated.

"You better start praying to someone a whole lot more powerful than some blue-eyed Mzungu, my friend. This isn't about me or pills at this point." I continued down the path. As I turned to step through the bushes and on to the trail, I peeked back. He was still sitting on the step, leaning forward, hands clasped and on his forehead. He was turning to a far better doctor than this planet could produce. Sarah, the little trooper with gangrene was next.

Several weeks of pills, then antibiotic lotions and then steroids were starting to make a difference. The odor was gone but the bumps and pustules were still there, just fewer in number. I scrubbed her leg again and opened the pustules with a rag soaked in hydrogen peroxide. A very large, silent crowd gathered. All I needed was a 500,000 Kilowatt spotlight and a gun to my head and I could have felt really comfortable. I worked in silence.

As I scrubbed and salved and worked on the dark little leg with the even darker patch of infection, I looked around the yard. I noticed a new structure that looked like a latrine. I also noticed a tippy-tap for washing the hands. Sarah's potential brush with death or loss of a leg had spurred the father to action. There are no atheists in foxholes.

"How you feeling, sweetie?"

After the translations I was told she was feeling better. She wasn't as tired anymore. She wasn't as hot either. I sensed a hurdle was being cleared but I wasn't going to say anything yet. I pushed all over the area of infection with my thumb. No response.

Standing, I handed the new ointment tubes to the father and gave him instructions. Again, this was a competent man. He could be trusted to perform the alternate treatments of antibiotic ointment followed a few hours later by steroids, followed by prayer. He agreed to the whole regimen. We all said a quick prayer and I left alone. On my way home, I passed three children with bulging abdomens. I had to suck it up. The reservoir was full.

Chapter Seventeen
Beyond Bicycles

At $30 used (junk) or $100 new, a bicycle is just a bit too expensive for most rural Kenyans. More than 90% of the bicycles are single-speed, unidentifiable makes that I believe are manufactured from rusty auto fenders. The most popular colors are rust or black with rust. Both come with a matching, oil-free chain which is completely dry and guaranteed to last for life if you define life as the time of use until the chain breaks on the death-highway to Kisumu.

I saw many men (women almost never ride bikes in Kenya) on the side of the road, clueless and tool-free, holding a heat-stretched chain in their hands.

More than 98% of the time, bicycles in the US are used for recreation and leisure. In Kenya, it's best not to think of them as bikes. Think of them as buses for three or more people, taxis for hire, and trucks for almost every imaginable article that can be transported by land. Kenyans have pluck and ingenuity. However, they have apparently no ability to conceive of the ceaseless pull of Earth's gravity. Many is the time I have seen several people picking up various portions of a previously bike-borne load while one of them does some form of grief counseling with the driver. I couldn't actually hear all of it but I think the counseling goes like this:

"I'm really hurt."

"Of course you are. I feel it too."

"My load of 6 coffins: two full, four empty is badly damaged."

"Life is a series of creation and destruction."

"Where do you get this drivel? I told you I am in great pain!"

"Remember, pain is just God's way of hurting you for being stupid."

Once while driving, I had to give way to a bike with a coffin on the back. It had a body in it and the cyclist was heading up a dirt road as I was driving down. We met at the part of the road where the water had gouged away most of the soil creating a model of the Grand Canyon. The coffin was spinning around on the back of the bike while the cyclist tried to steer the bike. A pair of older, would-be pall bearers rushed to his aid to help steady the load. I could tell they were in trouble and very rattled when they asked *me* for directions.

To date I have actually only seen three coffins stacked on one bike. Presumably, they were empty. However, I have seen 20 foot logs, six inches in diameter; crates stacked eight feet high; live chickens hanging by their feet from the driver, the seat and the handlebars; huge bags of tea billowing over the sides as the desperate driver pedals to the wholesaler ten miles away, trying to beat the rain.

I have seen a father and three children at 9:30 at night on the road from Kisumu being brushed by death's hand, just the fingertips, as car after speeding car passes within inches or fractions thereof. This is when it is no longer interesting or even cognitive. It is purely visceral but I could not identify the gut emotion as I looked at the strained faces of the father and the children, gripping him in terror. They repeat this ride, night after night. This father has two choices as I have pointed out before, bad and horrible. This was very, very bad.

I wonder what sentiments the mother has as she waits at home each night in a metal-roofed shed, anxious to know if she is the mother of a family of five or the widow in a family of one. What would she do in the middle of nowhere if she were suddenly all by herself? What will she do anyway?

Kids don't have bicycles. Some teens do when they begin work that requires transport. Bicycles are serious business. That's why I cannot understand why they won't put a drop or two of oil on the chains and hubs. Why be 40 kilometers from anywhere when your chain breaks or comes off the sprocket? I have looked closely at hundreds of bicycles. They all have the same rusty, dry chains. When it comes to maintenance, so far, no one blinks.

On one of my walks, I made the mistake I so often make of walking down the dirt path on the right side, just like an American. So a man riding his rusty bicycle at a fairly good clip had to pass me on the left. He glanced back at me to see if I looked as stupid as I behaved and as he did, he ran right over a dog that had just come through the bushes.

Thump! Yelp! Skid! Crash! He tore himself up pretty good from what I could see. He was bleeding through his pants but he didn't even look down at his leg. I was kind of concerned for the dog. He was most concerned for his bike. Wherever he was going, he could look disheveled and bloody but he had to have his bike. I later saw him as I drove past the neighboring town. He had gone twenty miles since rolling over Fido. He was still pedaling hard.

He recognized me as we passed by. He waved and smiled. No hard feelings from the morning, evidently. But I didn't ask the dog.

Chapter Eighteen
More on Husbands and Wives

I don't know why but I woke up a little after 2 AM one morning in the middle of my stay in Kenya. It was more than 2 hours before Satan's hired rooster hurled his fetid wail through the hole in my bedroom wall. So it wasn't anticipatory wakefulness like I get sometimes when I use an alarm clock. It was something else.

I had a momentary recollection of walking on a trail to one of my favorite hidden lakes in the North Cascades. My wife wanted to walk at a reasonable pace and I wanted to move quickly. She was miserable and I was frustrated. The reason God woke me up was to ask me why I was such a jerk. Walking fast or slow would change our arrival time by about 10 minutes for a three day stay. What was my hurry? It had a lot to do with showing my male prowess as a guy who could set records. To a guy, it's all about him. The first axiom of being a jerk.

It really bothered me that I had behaved that way. My wife never wanted to make that hike again. All I had to do was take it at her pace and enjoy the walk. It would have meant so much to her. But then it wouldn't have been all about me if I had let that happen. A lot can change in twenty years but you can't go back and undo the past. Men can really be jerks in any country. The men of Kenya just do it differently than the men of America.

We now know women are getting the proverbial short end of the stick when it comes to workload, legal standing, domestic disputes and the like. You should know that it gets worse from there.

I was in Mombassa being helped by a great store clerk at the Voyager Hotel where I was staying for a couple of days before flying home. I had finally found a country where people were shaped like me. The clerk was sorting through shirts that would fit me when the conversation turned to the subject of husband and wife physiques.

He stated that if there were a home where the husband looked like me with a thin waist but the wife had some extra weight on her, then it was probably a well run household. On the other hand, if the husband was thick around the middle and the wife was lean, that was clearly the sign of a poorly run family.

Now by poorly run, they don't mean procedurally well operated. Operating rectitude is the furthest thing from most African's consciousness. By well run, they mean fair and just. In a home where the husband eats well and the wife does not, everybody knows it's simply not fair. It means that although he's not working and she is; he is eating and she is not.

When I went to verify this position with the opinion of other Africans, I was shocked at both the speed and force of the response. Not only was it considered truer than gospel, but it had a number of twists to it as well.

Most agreed that a home where the husband becomes fat early in the marriage is a home that had a second wife soon after the first marriage. If the man eventually made it to a third and then a fourth wife, he was able to declare non-support for all the wives since it was beyond one man to provide for so many women and their children. He was off the hook. They were not. Each night he would have four dinners as each wife struggled to make sure her food was in keeping with the quality of the others. Serious consequence could come to the woman whose food was turned back or left uneaten.

But an early second wife does not necessarily mean there will be a third and then a fourth. I asked what happens if a man marries a woman who is not a good cook. Here's the narrative:

It depends. If she is otherwise of good character she still has other things to offer. Only the worst men will send her back home. It is however, commonly viewed as the fault of the mother and she is shamed for not teaching her daughter better. It is too late once she is married. At the time, the husband discovers she is a bad cook, he knows his future children will be raised in a home where they might become weak. He usually decides early that he must find a wife who cooks better.

So why isn't all this discussed and precluded ahead of time by the fiancée and her family? Because often there is no engagement period. The day the man and woman meet is often the day they decide to get married. On a tip from a friend or relative, he is directed to a prospective woman's home. It is always beyond the village borders, which might be too close genetically. He arrives by foot or by matatu and they talk. If it's a go, she puts her belongings and cooking utensils in a bag or two and they head back to his place. When she arrives they set up their household. They are now husband and wife.

She must toe the mark immediately. She knows then and forever thereafter, she can become unmarried just as fast as she became wife number 1 through 2, 3 or 4. Remember, this is a business arrangement he could dissolve at will. It's not like he's cutting some thick emotional tie.

Women have lousy odds anyway. But in a country where they have no land rights by custom, they are particularly vulnerable. I will likely be unable to make any changes nationally or across the African continent. But there are two things I can do on my end. I can really listen when my wife talks to me so I hear the music and the words. And I can do the best I can to raise my sons to recognize the tough position women are in even in America. I don't think we can fix this by legislation. That might make it worse. But a little individual leadership will go a long way.

Thinking about the hike and a number of other puffy things I had done, I went back to sleep with a little less than two hours before the rooster tortured the airwaves. I made a little vow to apologize to my wife abjectly and offer as an excuse -- absolutely nothing.

Chapter Nineteen
What Does Yes Mean?

Americans and most other English-speaking people have an interesting way of asking questions. We use the word "not" or its contraction in a question which is really asking exactly the opposite:

"Isn't that wonderful?"

"Won't you be staying here anyway?"

"Was that not one of the best dinners you have ever eaten?"

You need to be careful in Kenya because in Swahili and the Nilo-Sudanese family of languages, in general, a positive is used to confirm a question based on a negative supposition. Don't give up, I'll explain by example. This situation, which took place in a Nairobi restaurant, will also serve to preview why there will be inter-galactic war when the first spaceship lands.

After looking over the menu I asked the waiter, "Don't you have any vegetarian items on the menu?"
"Yes."

"Really? What do you have?"

"TiBONstek," he announced with the accent on the "bon" making it sound like Gabon, the African country. Now I was intrigued.
"That sounds different. What's in that?"

"Pardon, sir?"

"I meant, what do you cook it with?"

"The stove."

"OK, let me try again. What is it made with? You know ingredients, spices?"

"Oh, yes. The salt. It is made with the salt."

"Just salt? Isn't there anything else?"

Please note, this is another question based on the negative.

"Yes."

"I thought so. What else?"

"The chicken."

"The TiBONstek comes with chicken? Now that <u>isn't</u> very vegetarian is it?"

"Yes."

"It is? Well tell me, Ndugu, what are you calling vegetarian?"

"You are a vegetarian, sir."

"Yes. That's right. So I don't eat chicken."

"You don't want the chicken?" he asked me this time, using a negative supposition.

"No."

"So, I bring you the chicken?" I had unconfirmed his negative which in Swahili means he was wrong in his statement or question entirely.

Ok, I'll ask you a better question. Nitipata mboga nini hapa?" This is to say, "I will get vegetables, what kind, here?"

He listed several. I selected and ordered all side dishes, no entrée. He seemed relieved as he walked back to the kitchen.

Ten minutes later my vegetable arrived complete with baked chicken.

By the way, this is actually a little better than tiBONstek, which is better known in America as T-bone steak.

Chapter Twenty
Riverside thoughts

One morning I decided to go for my run before the sun started to peek over the distant hills. I was in need of some solitude – the solitude I was used to on morning runs where it was just the sound of my shoes tapping the dirt, my breathing and whatever thoughts God was willing to share with me. I laced my shoes with a degree of excitement. It wasn't that I didn't enjoy running with the school children, in fact I enjoyed the panoply of emotions arising from runners and onlookers. The air was always rich with feelings. Real feelings. But today, I just wanted to be alone with some of my own thinking.

By the time I had logged six miles or so, I heard the river calling me. Goal-oriented as always, I wanted to get my seven point five in before I stopped, but for once I heeded the call to a different goal. Turning off the main road, I started to make my way down ever narrower trails until I stood next to the river's edge. The night had dropped to fifty degrees and the mist was finishing the last dance on the top of the water as I seated myself and removed my shoes. I thanked God for this time alone and asked his blessing on the day for this village of people.

Prayers should be selfless, but I think God puts a burden on our hearts for other people. Mine was for a village that was fighting a battle and taking casualties. To relieve my own weight, I asked Him for a day free of pain and full of insight. Maybe that's His formula. He gets us all tied together and then to discharge the hurt, we pray for others for communal relief. It's a good plan.

As a kid I was drawn to lakes and rivers because I wanted to catch fish. Growing up, my family had only taken one vacation and it was by a river where we caught trout. I still have incredible memories of that warm summer, camped by ourselves, next to a river full of fish. I can still feel the rapid tug on the line and the excitement of reeling in a fish, mixed with a fear it would get away.

In other years, we had gone with my dad on business trips which mostly involved staying in motels and bouncing a ball in a parking lot while he called on a customer. On one such trip to Detroit, we sat in our car while my dad made a sales call. My mom, who had also grown up poor in Sedro Wooley, Washington, had hoped for more than this but she remained silent, a good sport all the way. Semper fi. As the temperature approached 90 degrees, she looked back at her three children overheating in the back seat and she slid over to the driver's seat.

"Let's go find a pool," she said as she started the car. We drove for almost forty-five minutes until we saw a sign for a public pool. She paid seventy-five cents for the three of us and we went in wearing our bathing suits. We were not prepared for what we saw. As we emerged from the drab green dressing rooms, we saw a large shallow pool, filled to the brim with black children. Not a single white kid in the lot. The pool went quiet until we dipped in and hung on the edge. Then the splashing and laughing resumed. We swam for only five minutes and then agreed that we should leave. Mom had tried, but it was just not a comfortable thing.

Now I sat as the lone Mzungu in a village of 7000 souls that had received me with open arms. I didn't feel the least out of place. I felt loved and respected. And needed.

The thin crackle of grass told me someone was coming to join me. I looked back and saw a woman in bare feet. Her hair was wet and her dark blue dress was newly pressed. She smiled as she approached.

"Hello, Mzungu. Cha-lees, right?"

"That's right, I'm Cha-lees. How are you today?"

"I am very good. Are you here to draw the river again?" Her English was actually pretty good.

"You mean measure? No, I'm here just to think. What brings you by so early?"

"I walked here because I saw you walk here."

"Well, it's nice to see you here. I was just praying."

"I should go and let you talk to God."

"No, I'm done for now."

She sat down on a rock and looked at the river. "Do you pray because you are sad?" she asked.

"No, I pray because I am trying to get some answers and because I want the people of Kodera to get better."

"You seem sad."

"Maybe I am. Three people died yesterday and I don't even know their names."

She told me their names and ages and a little history of each. That was just the way it was, she explained. People die.

"Kids don't die very often where I come from. It's not normal and you should never think it is normal. We could do so much to stop these people from dying."

"That would be good."

I then decided to ask her a question I had only gotten partial answers to - the question of women and their future. "What do you dream about?" I asked. She looked puzzled. So I changed the question a little. "What do you hope for? If thing get better, what will it look like for you and other women five years from now? What do you want to change? What would make life better for you?"

Her answers were the most distressing short lists of little wants: water abundance, food, pots and pans. Everything she mentioned improved slightly on exactly the same life she led. She never came up with a change in roles, advances in technology or availability of electricity or running water. She never talked about having more money. She just wanted to be able to do her chores better. My attempts at opening her eyes to bigger possibilities were met with dull stares. These were the fantasies of an outsider.

Soon, other people were joining us and the conversation with her broke off. We all then talked about small things. Pleasant things.

There was a good feeling all around. My first visitor seemed buoyed by the social event that was developing. Maybe this *is* what Utopia would look like if things got better. Maybe you finished your chores a little early and then you sat with good friends by the side of the river and just talked about pleasant subjects.

After a while, I got up to leave for home. We shook hands all around. Of course we shook hands. This was Luo land. I looked back at the party that had started. It was going to go for a while. Soon they would disperse and go about the day. They had chores to do that would take the women through nightfall.

On my way home, I finished my prayers. This time it wasn't for the people of Kodera. It was for all the people that had electricity and running water, big homes and big cars, everything. The only thing they did *not* have was a drought-restricted river that would draw friends to talk about nothing important. The center of their life was not God, it was their appetites. It was their pride. With pride you can't sit beside a weak river in a failing village and talk to unlettered people.

In Kenya, I had more conversations with more people about more topics in any given week than I have in three months in the US. I'm like everyone else, I have so much stuff, I don't need people. In fact, the last thing I dare show is that I *might* need people. Maybe that's what I liked most about Kenya. People needed me so I spent time with them. They needed my help in a lot of areas. I treated dozens of people for illnesses – some of which were life threatening. What I didn't figure out until the latter part of my stay, was that the medicine was welcome and perceived as vital but it was not the reason they always welcomed me. They just wanted another soul to talk to. Take away health, wealth and material success and all you have is each other. Maybe that's the place we should start.

Chapter Twenty-One
Animal Names of the Luo

Whereas Swahili borrows many of its words from Bantu and Arabic, Luo on the other hand goes right to the source. In the case of animal names and their sounds, all three million Luo share remarkably similar stories. The one about Oyango and the frogs turns out to be a common, humorous story. I did find out a week or so after I heard the story that the question being asked of old Oyango (who are you?) in Luo is pronounced "een nya" which doesn't sound like "rivet" but it does sound like the noise the local river frogs make.

The other creature that sort of "nya's" is the nga-nga; Luo for the glossy ibis, a large black bird about two feet in height with black feathers and a black bill. It flies around and issues the most comical cry of all the birds I heard in Kenya. It sounds like you are being mocked by the three stooges.

Here are a couple of animal stories to help you remember what to call the animals of Kenya:

The Donkey and the Zebra

Once there were two very dull looking animals of the plain, the donkey and the zebra. They spoke with one another and decided they needed to look more exciting. So they agreed to paint one another.

The donkey, being a good sport, got a gourd full of paint and proceeded to cover the zebra with a full set of stripes from its ears to its hooves. The zebra went to look in a water pool at his new exterior. He was so pleased he wanted to just show it off.

Now it was the donkey's turn to be painted. So the zebra came over, grabbed a brush, gave him one little stripe on the side of the head and ran off.

The donkey was upset and began to yell for him. To this day, all donkeys continue to yell for the zebra, "Magwar! Magwar!" The Luo name for Zebra is magwar even though it is the noise the donkey makes.

When I was doing the river measurements on the river running through Kodera, I got my first glimpse of the crowned crane. It's a tall, gorgeous bird with classy shades of designer blue colors. The head has a black fore crown that leads into stiff, spiky golden feathers that form a regal looking burst of a rear crown. The cheeks are bright white and the bill is black. There's a splash of red behind the eyes and along the throat. The neck is gray-blue and the body divides into blackish blue feathers in the upper area and whitish in the lower which leads to a black tail.

The day I saw them, approximately 20 had landed in a corn field near the river. This was a rare sight even for the villager I was with. Here's the crowned crane story:

The Crowned Crane and the Eagle

The crowned crane and the eagle once had a contest. They dug a wide pit and put burning logs in the bottom. They then challenged one another to stand on one edge and leap across to the other side without using their wings.

The crowned crane, a superb hopper, went first and cleared it easily. The eagle was next. He stood at the edge and looked down at the fire and then he looked across at the other side. He crouched and made his leap. He did not clear the pit and instead fell to the bottom of the pit and immediately caught fire.

Then the crowned crane began to shout to all who could hear, "Owang Ongo! Owang Ongo! Translated directly this means "He is burning, the eagle." This became the cry of the crowned crane from that time on. It is now shortened to "Ongo wan" the eagle burns. Ongo wan is the Luo name for crowned crane.

As you can see, among the Luo, there is no conflict between religion and science. They just go by what makes obvious sense.

According to several people I was sitting with, the most popular animal stories center around the rabbit. They asked me if I wanted to hear some. I applied my litmus test and asked in return if they were as good as the one about Oyango and Omol. They said they weren't as good but they were a lot longer. I asked if there were a shorter version They told me it wouldn't make sense if it was shorter.

"You mean, make sense like the zebra and donkey story?" I asked to get a metric for comparison.

"Yes," they said in unison.

As of this writing, I can say, possibly in some ignorance, that little rabbits come from big rabbits and that's all I know about rabbits.

Chapter Twenty-Two
A Cause for Hope

We had one more meeting before heading back to Nairobi. Two of the village men and I met with the new Director for the Ministry of Health for the Ranchyoro District of Nyanza Province. This had taken some real pushing and nagging on my part to get the villagers to set up this meeting. Unfortunately their last such meeting was a complete bust and very humiliating. Under former President Moi's regime of corruption, no official had any incentive to do anything for anyone. Pathetic villages like Kodera, despite a sizeable population, commanded no respect or interest. The last Director of Health had evidently told them this, talking out of the side of his mouth and rarely even looking up from his reading.

When we finally got through the screeners to meet with the Director, he asked some demographic and geographic questions and then invited me to tell my story. As I began, he listened intently for ten minutes and then stopped me. He called for one of his lieutenants who brought in a chair and joined us.

He asked the lieutenant some questions about clinic locations and then asked me to proceed. I told him what I had observed and what I was hoping he would do.

"We need enough worm medication to treat 7000 people – half of whom are children. We will need this once a quarter for a year."

"How would you go about getting the medicine to each of the people in the village?"

One of my companions intervened, "We can do it through the schools. We can go to each school and hand them out."

The Director turned to me and asked, "Will that work?" I suspected this was a test. "

No," I said firmly. "That won't even work for the children. It will likely miss everyone under five and the older children beyond primary school or who don't attend any school. Even primary school wasn't free under the Moi regime and a number of people in poor villages are unschooled. Whole families may be missed. Schools will be a means of allowing us to check progress, once the program has been applied."

"I agree," he said. "What do you propose?"

"We must divide the village up into sectors and then hand out the medicine in large teams of people who have been given a bit of training. We have to have all the names of all the people in the village."

"Can you do that?" he asked me but looked at my companions.

"We had better. The village of Jera has such a program north of Kisumu. We can replicate their process. Can you get us the medicine?"

"The medicine is no problem. There is plenty of medicine. Other villages have experienced the epidemic you describe. I agree with you, Mr. Herrick, it is making the children weak and opening them up to secondary infections. It is killing people." He then looked at my two confreres from Kodera. "Can you put such a plan together to hand out the medicine?"

They both looked at him blankly. My heart sank. No one is going to waste time or expensive medicine on a village that is not committed.

"We need help, Doctor. People are dying." I reiterated.

He continued staring at the two catatonics in front of him. Then he turned to me. "You need more than that."

"Such as…?" I asked, fearing the answer.

"You need a clinic." He turned to his lieutenant who had evidently been there under the Moi regime. This Director was planning to do a little undoing of the past. "Can you tell me," he demanded of his underling, "why a neighboring village which is only slightly larger than Kodera has six clinics and Kodera, with 25,000 souls between the three villages, has none?" I liked the word souls. This told me something about the man. But I knew the answer, dirty politics and rampant graft. I suspect he knew this as well.

"We were not made aware of the situation. This presentation has been very enlightening," one of the lieutenants oozed.

The Director turned to me. "We need to build a clinic in Kodera. Can your church organization help?"

"Yes. What kind of help would you like? We are a small group in Seattle but we are providing funds and education to get Kodera going economically. What else would you like us to do?"

"That will need to be worked out."

"Yeah, but you're thinking something. Can you give me a hint?"

"Equipment will be hard to come by. Can you get us some equipment?"

"Like X-ray machines and sonogram equipment?" I asked, knowing we were planning to get this for them anyway. In fact, we already had the sonogram.

"Yes. And lab equipment," he tacked on.

"The only way we can afford that is if some larger hospital upgrades old equipment." I needed to add a degree of difficulty or I would soon be adding bricks, cement and roof tiles to my side of the deal.

"Can you do it?" He wanted an answer not a contingency

"Yes."

"Now about the worm infestation," he continued. "You will need help. You need to talk to the Public Health deputy." (A Moi guy).

"Can you give him the word?" I requested. "It will help move things along." Without hesitation he picked up the phone. We drove over to a sheet metal shack in an storage yard for large road equipment.

This guy was sugary sweet. In the course of the conversation, he asked three times, "Did the Minister of Health really say we had plenty of medicine?" It was clear he had been cut out of an opportunity to get a little bribe or graft operation going. Under such an arrangement in the past, money exchanged hands and the medicine never got to where it was supposed to go. This was a slimy guy.

We left with a follow-up appointment set for one of the Kodera men who was with me. I would be gone. It looked like we were going to get the worm medicine we needed but it would be a fight. Three out of four children I saw had enlarged stomachs. Some were grotesquely huge. And this snake in the grass *Public Health* Deputy was willing to let that go on if he couldn't get his cut.

When we shook hands to leave I wanted to crush his reptilian fingers but this was not my domain. Cleaning up Dodge fell under the Genesis 41:16 charter. This man was only one of thousands of officials in government, churches and businesses who have long since given up any plans to be productive and have merely been seeking to get a slice without working for it. Let babies die.

Chapter Twenty-Three
Final Visits

It was a Sunday and all that morning, the yard had been criss-crossed by people going to churches of just about every denomination. I am amazed at how well people of different denominations in Kenya put aside non-dividing doctrines and just work together as Christians. I suppose if America ever finds itself in dire straits again like it was in World War II or the Great Depression, we will overlook sprinkling versus dunking baptisms and worshipping on Saturday versus Sunday. So what? James defines true religion in chapter 1: verses 26 and 27:

> *If anyone considers himself religious and yet does not keep a tight rein on his tongue, he deceives himself and his religion is worthless. Religion that God our Father accepts as pure and faultless is this: to look after orphans and widows in their distress and to keep oneself from being polluted by the world.*

That's why things are so much more spiritually grounded in Kenya. Proportionately speaking, they are way ahead of us on orphans and widows in distress.

Normally people came into our yard to stop and chat or join us for a meal. There were almost never prearrangements. Just friends being friends and people being people. But on Sunday, it seemed that people went out of their way to wander through one another's yards. They waved and said hello. This was God's day and they were going to celebrate his grace by sharing it with one another.

I had gone for a run earlier that day along my route to the school and back. I heard churches in session and I saw churches in session. The churches are constructed in the same manner as the homes. They are just shaped differently and typically they have a corrugated steel roof.

As IBM had moved us around the country, we had to find a new church in each new town we settled in. I avoided big worldly lukewarm churches and social clubs. But I have a confession: I also avoided shlubby little churches in bad settings. I was looking for baby bear.

In Kenya, churches are often located between a filling station and a junkyard. They are always marked by hand painted signs. In the villages, they are mud huts with stick windows. They are packed to the gunwales with the devout. Often I saw people leaning in from the outside through the windows. They wanted to worship. I never had to worry about being run over by fathers driving out of the parking lot to catch the opening kickoff because there were no cars or parking lots and there was no television. People in Kenya are stuck with a bunch of close friends, worshipping God in humble circumstances

Church used to be our big event in America. We worshipped God and uplifted our fellow man. People who were poor or of low station were usually, not always, on par with the other parishioners. Again James speaks to us in the second chapter of his epistle:

> *Suppose a man wearing a gold ring and fine clothes, and a poor man in shabby clothes also comes in. If you show special attention to the man wearing fine clothes and say, "Here's a good seat for you," but say to the poor man, "You stand there" or "You sit on the floor by my feet," have you not discriminated among yourselves and become judges with evil thoughts?*

As I passed by these churches on my run, I did not wonder how well attended a church with dirt floors and no windows would be in America. Judging by myself, I knew the answer.

In my last couple of days, it hit me hard. I was going to leave and these people, whom I had really come to love, were going to be back on their own. I watched women coming back from the springs with only half buckets. The drought had to end or it was going to kill many more. The insouciance they displayed was not mirrored in my face as I watched them head home to families of six and eight with only three gallons of water. I knew what that meant and so did they. So why was I the one who was so visibly dismayed? I think I know why.

I was leaving while the Pale Horse was still roaming the helpless village. There were two bad cases remaining and my last hours were going to be spent making sure I had done all I could do. That morning I had prayed a long prayer and I was reminded of the theme under which I had arrived in Kenya, Genesis 41:16's first four words, "I cannot do it…" followed shortly thereafter by "but God will."

The prayer was as much for myself as it was for the sick of Kodera. I did not want to leave with things unresolved. How could I just walk away from a spot of pneumonia or just a touch of gangrene which could work their way back into children who may not see a doctor for years? With a faith in God to handle things, I arose from kneeling, grabbed my little yellow kit and headed out to the mud homes down pathways now familiar to me.

I picked up my usual entourage – I still don't know how everybody could know I was coming. They would suddenly just be there. They joined me as I wandered in to see how Lisa's pneumonia was coming along. "Hodi, Hodi," I called out casually, expecting a quick "Karibu." But I heard nothing. There was a ringing quiet in the home. No one was there. A half dozen or so people had died lately. I had heard wailing, drum beats and ululations coming from every direction at all hours the night before. I didn't like this.

I turned to look at the men who had come with me. They were lolling about in the yard. No one would look at me. I clenched my jaw and walked to the edge of the property. Off to the side I heard a voice yell my Luo name, "Cha-lees." I looked and saw the woman who was now cured of her long term bladder and kidney infections as she waved to me. From out of the hedges darted a healthy little three-year old. It was Lisa. She criss-crossed the adjoining field as she screamed at the top of her lungs. She hadn't shown this much life in a long time.

Hand shakes and greetings with laughter went all around among an ever larger gathering of people. Everyone talked at once. If anyone thinks these people somehow get used to kids just dying and don't celebrate life everyday, they are missing what radiated through our little group that day. A tap at my back and I turned around to see my little patient step forward and do voluntarily what I had asked her to do so many times. Lisa stuck out her tongue and waited. This time it was pink, for the most part. She turned ninety degrees so I could listen to her lungs. I felt her forehead and smiled. She ran off to where two other young children were waiting and the three of them disappeared.

The father shook my hand solemnly. I told him I was leaving soon. I asked if Lisa had been taking her pills even though she was feeling well.

"Yes. This morning was last one."

"Well, good," I said reaching in my pocket, "Because here are two more days' worth. Did you tell her the story?"

"The weak bugs can come back," he recited, referring to the bacteria I had referred to as "little bugs you can't see."

"We want them dead and gone or so weak her body can kill them. Lisa just can't get sick again. I'm leaving."

"Okay."

"Did you finish that pit latrine?"

"I'll show you."

"I don't have time. I don't need to see it. Just tell me you will finish it and use it."

"Okay"

"You'll finish?"

"Okay"

I walked off with a sense of "maybe" lingering. When the storm has passed, the motivation to be prepared for the next one often isn't there. On to the next family.

Down the path, round the bend and through the hedge to the gangrene situation. Once again, neighbors came hurrying as they had done so many times at this particular home. Sarah knew to stand facing the sun, leg out. It looked great. There were a couple of minor bumps but the skin had dried - crinkled and tight. I asked a few questions and talked about ongoing care. I also asked about the sister with the ear infection and the brother with the painful worm tummy who had run screaming from the hut weeks before. All better.

The father asked if I could wait a minute. He ran inside and I heard paper rattling. He came back out with a kilo of jugery, the solid cone of molasses they make from squeezing sugar cane and boiling it down to thick syrup. He smiled and thanked me as he offered this gift of precious labor to me and then shook my hand with tears welling in his eyes. I felt like I had just won something. I had. Relief.

We talked about cleanliness and hygiene. I told him one more time, Sarah should go to Kisii hospital. He shook his head and said, "She is okay."

"I hope so. If it starts to come back, you must take her to the hospital."

"She is okay."

He was probably right and I felt his three-word summary was sufficient. Still, I would never acknowledge it aloud. I wanted my concerns to linger. Last words tend to do that and so do last silences.

It was time to go to Peter's hut. Once again, no one home. I looked around the clearing a bit and then I had to head back.

About a half mile up I heard the pounding of hard oxford shoes on dirt. It was Peter.

"Cha-lees. Cha-lees." He stopped me and caught his breath. We stared at one another for a moment.

"I'm leaving, Peter. I just stopped by to see how you and your family have been doing."

"We are very, very good. Everybody is good. Very good."

"The ear infection is gone?"

"Yes. Gone. Very good."

"How about the little guy's cough?"

"All good. Very good. You are leaving?"

"Yes, Peter. I hate to go but I have to go back to my family now. It's been a long time."

"You will come back?"

"I want to. If it's God's will, I'll be back again."

With tears in his eyes he told me once again, how good everybody felt. They had all been sickly a long time; so long they had forgotten what it felt like to be well.

In silence, Peter and I walked the rest of the way to my dwelling. He shook my hand again and then left. I really liked Peter. He had a lot of character and a huge African smile that always brightened my day. I turned to go into my yard. I looked back as he walked down the long road to his mud hut. I wiped the tears away and shook off thinking what kind of life he was heading back to. Memories of the whole family emerging from around the divider in that dim little dirt-floored shack still seemed so inconceivable to me. I know how they get seventeen rodeo clowns to emerge from a VW bug but I don't know how that family did it. But for now at least, they are healthy sardines.

I had hoped for a promising sign. I had prayed for relief. I never expected a 100% cure rate. What an incredible blessing. My eyes overflow with tears as I write this. It was all just so awful and so wonderful - all twisted together and wrapped tightly around my sun-bleached spirit.

As I drove out of the village, I slowly passed the general area of each of the homes and looked for signs of life. I couldn't see anyone. As I finally passed the house with the girl who had had gangrene, I looked for Sarah but saw nothing. Then something caused me to look in the opposite direction. There she was. She was standing in the shade, leaning against a support post on a shack across the road from her family's home. She held her hands behind her back as she leaned and watched me in silence. She still wore that one raggy dress, with the loops and tatters. It used to be orange but was now a dirty faded pink.

I waved good-bye to her. She didn't wave back but, while still leaning against the post, she casually stuck her leg out one last time - into the bright midday sun.

Treating gangrene in the early days of my stay.

Sarah trusted me. I trusted God — but I still wore rubber gloves.

She was a remarkable little girl.

The last scene. Taken as I crossed the river in Kodera on the way out of the village. Upstream the cattle are wading in to get out of the heat. Downstream, a woman is washing clothes. I spent so much time by this river and I met so many of the people who are sharing this time on earth. I'll always have great memories of this nameless tributary.

Thirty years from now, I'll look at this picture and I'll believe these boys are still splashing around like young boys do. The little girl I treated for pneumonia will still be three years old and healthy. The mirror won't let me escape my own reality but if that reality will kindly allow me to keep these people forever young in my mind, then I'll just be a little more careful to enjoy each sunset and things will be ok.

Chapter Twenty-Four
Nairobi Again

It was amazing how good Nairobi now looked to me. Someone must have really worked hard on cleaning it up because it did not look nearly as dark and dusty as it did on my first day in Kenya. Maybe it was just tired, if a city can get tired. Maybe it just needed a rest.

I had a little extra time during the day so I drove out to the nicer suburbs for a visit to Karen Blixen's homestead. She was the author who wrote several books including "Out of Africa" which was made into a movie. Having once owned a coffee company and because I love that particular time in history, I was excited about seeing her place - an old coffee plantation.

Prior to arriving there, I stopped at a rustic little restaurant that was a restored ranch house from the Blixen era. It had a nice veranda where I ordered some Kenyan coffee served in a French press pot. As I sipped my coffee, I heard a sound I hadn't heard for a long time, coming from inside the restaurant. It was an espresso machine. I called the waiter over to my table.

"Is that an espresso machine I hear? I would really like an Americano."

He hesitated. "We can make you a latte."

"If you can make me a latte, then you can make me an Americano."

Again, he hesitated. "Look," I said, "I once owned a coffee company. If you guys don't know how to make an Americano, I'll be glad to teach you."

He brightened right up. "We would really like that. We get the request so often but we have no idea what it is or how to make it."

"Let's go inside. It's the easiest espresso drink in the world."

They had no idea what the short second wand was for on the machine. I taught them how to adjust their grind because the espresso shots they were making were awful. They then made a couple of crema-topped shots and I watched as they laughed and competed with one another. Next, I added the hot water from the wand they thought was broken since it spat instead of steaming. It's commonly called an Americano wand. It's not supposed to steam.

I made a bunch of friends, had a great Americano and got a really good discount on all my coffee that morning.

Next I went over to the Blixen place just down the road. It was very modest and charming. The leather, metal, wood and cotton that made up all furnishings, equipment and clothing caused the nostalgic twinge in me that it always does. I'm reminded each time I see such a place that I was born about a hundred years too late. What an era.

I walked into her back yard, which was much diminished now to accommodate nearby growth. Sitting on the dry lawn with my knees pulled up next to my chin, I stared at her veranda. I could see myself seated there with a white shirt, khaki trousers and a canvas belt, which just happened to be what I was wearing. I could see myself looking out over the dry grass and past the acacias. I closed my eyes to visions of a similar scene less than a month old from when I was lying in a hammock in the midday sun, smelling the grass bake, watching the warthogs joust and scurry on the Serengeti.

I couldn't help but think that it should still be that way. Not just to satisfy my displaced nostalgia. But because what I saw all around me was no improvement on what once was. Dead grass and dusty warthogs are better than sidewalks and matatus. Stiff little tails are way better than smoking tailpipes. Still, I'm a realist, sort of. I let go.

The drive to Jomo Kenyatta Airport that night took me along the main road through the city and out of town. Sinister looking Marabou storks by the hundreds glared at me as we drove under the trees and overpasses where they would spend the night. They were my final figurative reminder that evil still has plenty of places to perch in Kenya.

My flight was scheduled for 11:35 PM. It was running late and I would not be taking off until after midnight. Passengers sat waiting for the plane in a grubby little gate area. There was standing room only. But something was different. I think it was me.

One after another, babies began to cry. Soon eight were crying. Not long ago, even one crying baby would have irritated me and made me wonder why the mother wasn't doing a better job. Now, I just felt sorry for these mothers and their tired little babies. I wasn't the least bit irritated.

Our flight went north through the Sudan and the lifeless Sahara. As we reached the shore of the Mediterranean I glanced back for as long as I could get an angle. I knew I would be back, whoever I now was. I say that because this was just too much. Death and sunshine, bloated babies and sugar cane groupies, dead Zebras, frightened bicyclists pumping rusty old bikes past tired young women in the middle of the night. All this was running through one fuse in my little white brain. It was just too much. It's still too much. I will never look at life the same way again.

Chapter Twenty-Five
Home

The human capacity to suppress reality was something I was aware of but I don't recall experiencing it prior to my return home from Kenya.

When the plane arrived in Amsterdam I checked the telemonitors to see if my flight to Seattle was on time. It had been cancelled. I asked the woman at the transfer desk what Plan B was looking like. She explained there was no Plan B.

"Your president has plans for the whole world so a lot of flights are getting cancelled."

"Thank you for your polemical approach to flight scheduling. Can you tell me something useful that will get me home?" I was tired.

"You need to go over to the customer service desk down the next concourse."

I thanked her and walked over as she had directed to the next concourse. A quarter of a mile later, I was standing in line while a woman I recognized from the Nairobi airport was conferring with the lone ticket agent. The conversation seemed like it was going into extra innings when I noticed she finished her drink and, without looking, reached over and dropped the iced cup on the floor. This had to have been a mistake, I thought. A minute later, she wadded her napkin into a ball and dropped it in the same place as the spent drink. The Europeans and I all looked at each other without any idea of a solution to a problem that one should never encounter this side of the Twilight Zone.

When it was my turn to step up to the counter, a couple of additional agents had arrived. I told her what had happened to my flight. I also suggested that as an American who had just spent a lot of money to fly on her company's airplanes that her colleague at the transfer desk should be more understanding and less political.

"Well what do you expect her to do?"

"Keep her mouth shut about politics and talk to me about airplanes." Did I mention I was tired?

"I believe it's not so much a question of politics to some people as it is a question of morality."

"Well that reminds me, do I have enough time during this stopover to go to your legal red light district and have an illicit rendezvous and buy some legalized heroin?"

"What can I do for you, sir?" she asked, ignoring my comment.

"I want to go to Seattle as quickly as I can and I would like to use your phone to call my wife and tell her that my arrival will be delayed."

"Anything else?"

"Yeah, I want to tell her that I love her and while I was crawling around in mud huts and drinking out of ditches, I thought about her a lot. Does that get me a phone call home?"

"I meant is there anything else I need to do to help you at this point?"

"You can dial the number and accept my sincerest appreciation."

Without hesitation, she picked up the phone and called an operator. She relayed my home number and then handed the phone back to me. "It's ringing."

I got the answering machine.

"I'm sorry, sir," she said as she reached for the receiver.

"Can you try again? She'll get it this time. That's how it works at our house. I don't know why."

She tried again and soon I was talking to my wife. Then I wasn't. It all seemed surreal.

"Why were you crawling around in mud huts and drinking from ditches?" She asked with genuine interest. I told her briefly about where I was as she filled out my new ticket. She didn't say much at first but when she handed the tickets to me she thanked me and apologized for the political stuff.

"That's ok," I offered. "It wasn't long ago that it was a big thing with me, too. Things just changed somehow. I'm not upset and I appreciate the way you have accommodated me."

Soon I was in the gate area. Someone asked me where I was coming from. Within a couple of minutes, half of the crowd of people waiting to board were gathered around listening and asking questions. It turns out that life in Kenya was foreign even to foreigners.

On each leg of the flight I ended up sitting next to people who were deeply interested in Kenya. Any attempt to ask them about what they were doing overseas was answered briefly and then it was back to Kenya. I soon found that I could not talk about some of the people there, especially the children who were so sick, without the tears flowing. I still can't.

I arrived home after being picked up at the airport by my wife and wonderful daughter who will never know how much I missed them. They will also never know how glad I am that they had not been where I had been. It was vividly beautiful, tough the way I like things to be now and then and I guess the other psychometric dimension would be raw – as red-raw as the marbled, warm carcasses of the goats in the open air butchery near Kisii.

One last recollection and then I'm done. I normally sleep only four hours per night - a fact which disturbed the Kenyans almost as much as my vegetarianism. However, after coming home, I slept almost 18 hours a day for the first three days. And I remember waking up in the middle of the afternoon on the second day back. I sat up in bed, completely unable to make sense of where I was. I looked out over our pasture and tried to think what village or town I was in. I was disturbed that I was still in Kenya. I thought I had made it home but I guessed I hadn't and I really wanted to be home.

I wanted to be away from something there in Kenya but I don't know what it was. Whatever it was, I wasn't frightened for myself but something told me that a lot of people were in trouble. Even as I turned my head and looked about my room, I couldn't shake the sense that I wasn't all the way home yet. One slip or wrong turn and I was going to still be there. It was an hour at least before it quit bothering me so.

I sought out Kristy and held her close. She likes to be held. I held her because I love her. I gave her a hug to feel the reality that I was really home and then I held her for all those women in Africa who never get held the way they should. Ever.

Epilogue

Anything profound I could share at this moment, would only take away from what I now hold inside me. Some of it I will never let out. On my last drive to Nairobi I was hit by a flood of memories. As my personal epilogue, I wrote the following poem:

OF KENYA

Women walk highways under a load
Hot babies are nursed right next to the road
And cattle pass by unfazed by the goad
These are the road signs of Kenya

Where women are bent with the adz breaking soil
Or patiently waiting for dinner to boil
As husbands move loads on bikes thirsty for oil
These are the workings of Kenya

A market that's covered with dirt and debris
A classroom of farm children under a tree
A hospital single bed now holding three
This is what's public in Kenya

A butcher's goat, warm, fly-ridden and raw
A tree turned to lumber with a simple hand saw
A purse snatcher killed in sight of the law
This is the business of Kenya

A child's simple scratch turns into gangrene
A wife dies of AIDS and she's only sixteen
A one-legged woman still poised and serene
As she follows and haunts me from Kenya

Then barefooted neighbors come walk through your land
Toward mudden church houses with no room to stand
Sincerest of greetings; the grasp of a hand
These hold firm my memories of Kenya.